SALADS
COOKBOOK

Good Cook's Library

SALADS
COOKBOOK

Annette Wolter

Crescent Books
New York

Published originally under the title Salate,
by Gräfe und Unzer GmbH, München
Copyright © 1988 Gräfe und Unzer GmbH, München

English translation copyright © 1989 by Ottenheimer Publishers, Inc.

Text by Annette Wolter
Photographs by Odette Teubner

ISBN: 0-517-67104-2
h g f e d c b a

Contents

About this Book

Gourmets and those conscious of healthy eating habits like to eat salad. Variety is desired. Therefore, a wide range of exciting salads is presented in this richly illustrated cookbook — salads to satisfy any palate. The recipes offer diet-conscious meals as well as dishes for special occasions. Extraordinary creations, satisfying meals and, above all, easily prepared salads are all included. The collection takes note of trends, brings in ideas of "bistro-cuisine," and combines old favorites with interesting new salads. The striking color photographs, made exclusively for this book, show just how varied salads can be, every dish is pictured. Novices will enjoy success right from the start with these uncomplicated recipes.

Information on preparation and cooking times makes sensible planning easier. Special comments are provided to indicate if a recipe can be made quickly or if it takes time, whether it's economical or relatively expensive, whether it's easy to prepare or a little more difficult. Also, these remarks refer to famous recipes, specialties, or if the dish is a meal in itself.

Dressings add so much to salads. Oil and vinegar are the most important partners to a salad. Therefore, an overview of these salad complements is also given so that the cook will learn what foods go best with olive oil, linseed oil, pumpkin-seed oil, or walnut oil.
With vinegars, it all depends on the refined aromas. Find out what kinds of vinegars are recommended for particular kinds of dressings. Apple-cider vinegar, balsamic vinegar and sherry vinegar are described in this section.
Since shopping for the right ingredients is so important, a section is provided explaining ingredients to look for and how to keep them at their best. Color step-by-step photos show how to make favorite dressings like vinaigrette, cream-lemon, French dressing or homemade mayonnaise. The most common and important steps for making any salad are explained in the same way.

The recipe section begins with a chapter on "Appetizer Salads." Here suggestions are found for cocktails with artichokes, shrimp, mussels, lobster, quail eggs and even tofu. Also, included are sophisticated combinations with breast of goose, smoked salmon, trout fillet, crabs, or feta cheese. Not forgotten are well-known combinations of leafy salads and vegetables, with fresh herbs, with grain or with sprouts.
Then the chapter "Favorite Side Dish Salads" follows in both familiar and surprising forms. Choose from celery-walnut, kohlrabi salad with beansprouts, leek with bacon, radishes with Roquefort dressing, mushroom with watercress, or dandelion with green rye. This chapter leads one through all four seasons and takes the most varied nuances of taste into account.
To make meals out of salads, then look for many suggestions in the chapter "Salads as Meals." Italian salad, Greek salad, or beef salad with red beets probably are among the favorite recipes. Recipes for salads of vegetarian cuisine are also included, like lentil salad or millet-vegetable, as well as classic potato, rice and pasta salads, all combined with fresh ingredients.
The last recipe chapter is devoted to "Party Salads." These recipes were all conceived for eight people, many are easily prepared, all contribute to a successful party. The cook and the guest will be thrilled by these deliciously new creations.

One last word on the health aspect of salads. They don't just taste exceptionally good and fresh. From a nutritional perspective, they offer many advantages: they contain important vitamins, minerals, trace elements, and fiber.
With this book, any cook will always be able to conjure up something healthy and culinarily interesting.

Enjoy trying these recipes and bon appetit!

Please note that unless otherwise stated, all recipes are for four people.

he Value of Salad

Even the earliest cultures knew that herbs and vegetables made people feel better. The knowledge of many plants was handed down by learned monks, who came by the seeds for their cloister gardens by way of their wide contacts. Today there is great awareness of how healthy salad is and that it belongs in the daily regimen, nevertheless, people are relatively careless about the regularity with which they eat salad, as well as shopping for the ingredients and preparing the salads they do eat.

Nutritional Value and Quality

Any salad is only as good as the quality of all its ingredients. First choice should always go to native plants from the closest sources, using organically grown ingredients whenever possible. If the available material is seasonally limited, then one should use imported plants or sprouts and fresh herbs to improve nutritional value and variety. Leafy greens, herbs, and vegetables should be used freshly harvested, since these foods hold essential substances like vitamins, minerals and trace elements, which can only be gotten by eating. These substances are destroyed by storage or improper handling, since they are often highly sensitive to exposure to oxygen, light, or heat. The ingredients in the dressing should also meet the highest standards. Spices must not have lost their flavor, the kernels or seeds should be ground or milled only shortly before use. Herbs should be chopped and added to a salad shortly before serving.

Fresh Food

Today we use the term "fresh food" to replace the term "raw food," which has negative connotations for many people. Nutritional experts advise beginning

every meal with fresh food — a dish of uncooked vegetables of high quality. Since nutritional value is so sensitive to heat, only raw ingredients offer the maximum of essential nutritional substances. A selection of plants that grow in and above the soil are recommended: leafy vegetables, fruits, cabbages, sprouts and stalky plants mixed with roots and tubers. These plants only need be cut or chopped after washing; all edible parts are used, including roots, stems, leaves, buds and seeds. The skin and peel as well as kernels and other, often unpopular, harder parts contain valuable nutritional elements and are high in fiber. Some vegetables like green beans are not acceptable for raw ingestion, because they contain indigestible substances which are destroyed only by cooking. Potatoes are not eaten raw because their starch is edible only after cooking.

Variety of Salads

Besides a wide selection of leafy salads, various types of fruits and vegetables are available (raw, quickly cooked, or blanched), as well as meat, fish, seafood, cheese, eggs, and rice, noodles or grains.

Salads and Dressings

The dressing is the soul of a salad! The connoisseur lays a great value on a delicious dressing.

Here is the rule of thumb for a balanced relationship of the ingredients of any dressing: one part vinegar, spices, four parts oil, herbs. Vinegar and oil can be replaced by lemon juice and cream, crème fraîche, yogurt or cream cheese.

After combining the salad with the dressing in a large bowl, it should be put in a glass, ceramic or porcelain serving bowl. Wooden vessels are not a good idea, because they can never be thoroughly cleaned and they often smell somewhat rancid after long use. Leafy salads should be served immediately after combining the ingredients,

since the oil softens the delicate leaves. If a leafy salad has to be made ahead of time, then one should mix it with the dressing minus the oil, dribble the oil on right before serving, and toss the salad. Salads made of firmer stuff should be allowed to sit covered at room temperature for 15 to 30 minutes. Crudités uncooked vegetables and leafy salads, are cut into pieces and arranged on a platter. A vinaigrette sauce or a variety of dressings are offered separately. Salad dressings can be spiced according to inclination or what is available. Besides salt and freshly ground pepper, familiar spices are also appropriate, but do not forget cognac, yeast extract or yeast flakes, garlic, horseradish, any mustards or ground mustard seeds, roasted sesame seeds, sherry, soy sauce, tomato paste, wine, or onions. For just a trace of garlic flavor, rub the salad bowl with a clove of garlic. For a sweet-and-sour note, rather than sugar, try acorn syrup, apple or pear concentrate, honey, ketchup, mango-chutney, or raw sugar.

Decorating Salads

Anything goes, as long as the flavors are appropriate. Naturally, carefully dicing the ingredients or cutting them into strips or rings accurately will do a lot to make a salad look good. A lot of ideas are found from just looking at the illustrations in this book.

Oil and Vinegar

Oil

The word oil is derived from the Latin *oliva* for olive, since this is where the ancients got their oil. However, this much sought after product can come from many other sources, like seeds and fruits. In choosing an oil, one must be as careful about the flavor of the source as one is about the means of production. Oil can be pressed or extracted. In extraction, the oil is drawn from the mashed and heated raw product by means of a solvent, then the solvent is removed by distillation. This can produce a large volume of oil, but the oil must be refined. In this process, the oil is de-acidified, bleached, filtered, and results in a product which is neutral in flavor, keeps well, and can stand high heat, since all other organic elements have been removed. Hot pressing results in a similar product. For salads, however, recommended is a product which most closely resembles its raw source and which retains the nutritious valuable fatty substances. This oil can only come from freshly harvested, cold-pressed produce. This method produces far less oil which means it is more expensive. Cold-pressed, unrefined oil must be stored in a cool, dark place and should be used up quickly once the seal is broken. It has been filtered and slightly heated in order to remove harmful by-products, but the remaining fatty substances can cause it to become rancid. Cold-pressed, unrefined oil contains unsaturated and polyunsaturated fats, which the body needs since it cannot produce them itself. This oil also contains vitamin E, lecithin, phosphates, and stearins.

The following cold-pressed, unrefined oils are recommended for salads because of their nutritional value and aromatic flavor:

Naturally pure olive oil
It tastes mildly spicy. If it is from the first pressing, it is golden-green in color and is called virgin oil. The Italians call it "olio extra vergine," the French "extra vierge." It is a little less expensive. If it comes from the second cold pressing it is thinner, stronger in flavor, and greener. It is also an extraordinarily fine oil and is marked as cold-pressed, extra, fine, and middle fine.

Safflower seed oil
Produced from the seed of the safflower, it is an especially valuable oil, which is rich in fatty acids and spicy in flavor.

Linseed oil
Linseed oil, made from the seed of flax, is also very fine and especially savory in flavor. Pressed linseed oil has a yellowish-green color, extracted oil is yellowish-golden to dark red.

Pumpkin seed oil
This oil is developed from speci... pumpkins. It has a nutty flavor, dark-green or violet in color, an... is considered a delicacy.

Soybean oil
Made from soybeans, it is clear in color and tasteless.

Sunflower seed oil
Cold-pressed from sunflower seeds, it is highly nutritious and mild in flavor.

Wheat seed oil
Made from the seeds of ripe wheat, it contains vitamin E and B-complex vitamins. It is considered a good oil for dieters. Its fine grain flavor gives salads a sophisticated note.

Walnut oil
This specialty from the Perigord is produced only by cold-pressing. It has the finest aroma and contains many nutrients.

Vinegar

Vinegar is considered a healthy spice. It is made from alcohol and airborne vinegar bacteria. If a bottle of wine were left standing open, the vinegar bacteria would turn the alcohol into acid. A vinegar made this way is not very stable and would soon spoil, becoming cloudy and losing its aroma. That is why homemade vinegar should be used quickly and all vinegar should be stored in a closed bottle in a cool, dark place. Vinegar whets the appetite, its acid helps break down fat and carbohydrates, and helps in digesting proteins. The fine aromatics of different vinegars lend flavors to dishes.

Apple vinegar

Apple wine or cider is usually the raw product. It is popular for its light apple flavor. The vinegars made with honey or honey and whey are particularly mild. The intense French apple vinegar is made from cider apples.

Balsamic vinegar

Aceto balsamico

This fine Italian vinegar is expensive, since it must age for some time — up to six years — in wooden casks. The older the vintage, the more expensive the product. Only a few drops are needed to get the distinctive aroma and flavor.

Brandy vinegar

This is the base for many aromatic vinegars. It is made from grain or potatoes. Pure potato vinegar is mild and actually quite nice without any additional flavor. Concentrated alcohol from grain is turned into vinegar and most often used for herbal vinegars.

Malt vinegar

This is an English specialty, very carefully produced from beer. Malt barley, fermented to beer, must ferment longer in special steel barrels with beech staves. Caramel is added after bottling to give the vinegar a color similar to malt. It has a distinctive, pleasant aroma and is an ingredient of Worcestershire sauce.

Wine vinegar

"Real wine vinegar" is made from red or white wine with a high alcohol content. The more intensive acid is diluted to about 6% by the addition of water. Making it takes a long time, but the product is of highest quality, hence the high price.

Sherry vinegar

High quality sherry vinegar is made from the sherry of Jerez, Spain. In its pure form, it is a delicacy. It should always be used sparingly. Read the label carefully before you buy; there are vinegars that contain some sherry vinegar, but their main ingredients are herbal essences. These do not compare with the real thing.

Spice Ideas for Vinegar and Oil

To spice and flavor vinegars and oils according to individual tastes, use bottles that close tightly and cold-pressed oil or a neutrally flavored vinegar.

Rosemary oil

Three sprigs of fresh rosemary should be rinsed, dried, and allowed to air-dry for a few hours. Put the sprigs in a bottle tall enough to hold them and pour in enough oil to cover them. Cork the bottle and let it stand in the refrigerator for 14 days. Use the oil for dressing, but always pour in enough fresh oil to cover the herbs again. Basil oil, lavender oil, sage oil, or thyme oil can be made the same way. Homemade oils should be used in less than 6 weeks.

Lemon Vinegar

Combine the thinly sliced rind of one lemon, 5 tablespoons freshly pressed lemon juice, 1 cup wine vinegar, and 4 leaves of lemon balm in a bottle. Close the bottle tightly and allow to stand refrigerated for at least 3 weeks.

Homemade Salad Dressings

Vinaigrette Sauce

Its name is derived from the French word *vinaigre* (vinegar). This dressing is tart and spiced with all kinds of herbs. The quality of the vinegar used here will play a large role. Italian balsamic vinegar is well suited for all salads with Mediterranean lettuces; apple cider vinegar works better with salads that are strong flavored; and white wine vinegar is best for fruit salads with delicate flavors.

For 4 portions chop 4 sprigs of fresh tarragon, a well as chervil, chive, fres parsley, and 2 shallots.

Mayonnaise

Salad mayonnaise usually consists of 50% fat. Connoisseurs like to make it themselves, although that can be difficult, since all ingredients have to be at exactly the same temperature (room temperature is best), so that the mayonnaise does not separate.

For 4 portions, separate th yolk from 2 eggs.

Lemon-Cream Dressing

The pleasantly tart flavor of this velvety dressing goes well with all leafy lettuces, with asparagus, sweet peas, celery, and mixed vegetables. To moderate the tartness, adding ½ teaspoon sugar dissolved in the lemon juice will help. Important: Pour the cream into the juice in a thin stream under constant even stirring with a whisk.

Blend the freshly pressed juice of 1 lemon with ½ teaspoon salt and one goo pinch of freshly ground white pepper, until the sal is dissolved.

Mango Dressing

A creamy and fruity salad dressing which complements nobler ingredients like fish, shrimp, crab, or lobster, but does just as well with leafy salads. These salads can be combined with hard-boiled eggs, peas, corn, or mushrooms, or add poultry or ham to lettuce.

Peel one ripe mango, cut into wedges, dice the wedges and mix with 2 tea spoons lemon juice.

Blend ½ teaspoon salt and 1 dash of freshly ground white pepper with 2 tablespoons white wine vinegar until salt is completely dissolved.

Combine 4-5 tablespoons of flavorless oil with the herbs and shallots. If desired, add some crushed garlic.

Blend the yolks with ½ teaspoon salt, a pinch of freshly ground white pepper and 1 tablespoon mild vinegar until the mixture is smooth. Add 10 tablespoons oil, at first drop by drop, then in a very thin stream.

Important: Always stir evenly, so that a homogeneous, white sauce results. If a fatty film remains on top, add a few drops of lukewarm water.

Whisk 7 oz. cream into the lemon juice, pouring the cream in a thin stream. The dressing will get more and more velvety while it is whisked.

Whisk the dressing to a smooth cream. Serve the dressing separate from the salad.

Heat and dissolve 2 teaspoons honey in a little orange juice and blend with a pinch of salt, 1 teaspoon mild mustard and 6 tablespoons cream.

Blend 2 tablespoons cream cheese with the honey-cream and stir in the diced mango. Flavor to taste with salt, mustard and a little honey.

Homemade Salad Dressings

Thousand Island Dressing

Light salad mayonnaise forms the base for this fantastic dressing. It is actually a finished product, but you can give it a flavorful twist any way you like. It is well suited to mixed salads, as well as fish and poultry salads.

Finely chop 1 small pickle. Peel and grate ½ of a small shallot.

Herb-Yogurt Dressing

Refreshing, light and nutritious, this dressing is suited for all fresh salads all through the year.

Wash, dry, and chop basil, dill, chervil, parsley, rosemary, chive, and thyme.

Dijon Dressing

Use a moderate dosage of mustard for this savory hot dressing. It all depends on individual tastes, if the mustard should dominate, or if the dressing should be toned down a little. Either blend in a little more mustard, or make the dressing milder by adding a little sugar.

Pulverize 7 blond mustard seeds and 2 white peppercorns with a mortar and pestle.

Roquefort Dressing

The flavor of Roquefort cheese dominates this salad dressing. It conveys a sophisticated spiciness to salads of delicate flavor like avocados, chicory, corn, and zucchini. But it is also quite tasty with celery, cucumbers, or tomatoes.

Blend 2 oz. Roquefort cheese and 3 tablespoons cream with a fork to a smooth mass.

Bake ¼ of a bell pepper until the skin blisters. Remove the skin and seeds and finely chop the pepper.

Press 2 hard-boiled egg yolks through a sieve. Blend with 2 oz. salad mayonnaise, 3 tablespoons cream and 3 tablespoons ketchup, a pinch of salt and a pinch of chili powder, the chopped pickle, bell pepper and the grated shallot.

Peel 1 onion and 1 garlic clove. Finely chop the onion. Press the garlic through a garlic press into the chopped onion.

Blend 4 oz. light yogurt with the herbs, onion, and 5 oz. cream. Add salt and freshly ground white pepper to taste.

Blend 1 tablespoon Dijon mustard with 1 teaspoon white wine vinegar, ½ teaspoon sugar, and the pulverized ingredients.

Beat 5 oz. crème fraîche with 1 pinch of salt and 1 egg yolk until creamy and blend with the mustard mixture.

Blend 2 oz. cream cheese with 1 tablespoon white wine vinegar and 2 tablespoons dry white wine.

Whisk both cheese mixtures together until creamy. If necessary, add a little cold chicken broth (with fat removed), to thin.

Homemade Salad Dressings

French Dressing

A dressing that suits all crisp or leafy salads in all seasons. Also goes well with cucumber, tomatoes, zucchini, or cooked green beans. Depending on the salad, freshly chopped onion can be added to the dressing.

Blend 2 tablespoons lemon juice with 2 pinches each salt, freshly ground black pepper, mustard powder, and ½ teaspoon sugar until the sugar and salt are thoroughly dissolved.

Apple-Horseradish Dressing

This Austrian specialty often accompanies cooked beef as a puree. When thinned to a salad dressing, it is tasty in salads with a piquant flavor of their own, like watercress, or combinations with celery, red cabbage, spinach, sorrel, or even cooked beef or pickled pork.

Peel and grate 2 apples that are not too sour.

Italian Salad Dressing

This dressing conveys that typically Italian combination of virgin olive oil and basil. While there are several versions of this recipe, the following recipe is served with garden salad and tomatoes.

Peel and grate 2 small shallots. Finely chop about 2 tablespoons of fresh basil.

Cocktail Dressing

This delicate dressing with a mayonnaise base is particularly tasty with elegant cocktails, especially fine appetizer salads which are served in cocktail glasses. Seafood, fine fish, game and game birds, white poultry meat or roast are quite nice with slightly sweet-and-sour fruits, with mushrooms, or with eggs.

Peel and grate 1 small apple and combine with 1 tablespoon lemon juice.

Fold 5 tablespoons virgin olive or walnut oil into the prepared mixture with a whisk.

Cut about 2 tablespoons chives into the dressing and toss with salad.

Peel, wash and grate a 3—4 inch piece of horseradish and combine with the grated apple and 2 tablespoons lemon juice.

Salt and sugar to taste. Blend with enough naturally cloudy apple juice to make a velvety sauce.

Blend 3 tablespoons dry white wine and 1 tablespoon white wine vinegar with 1 pinch each salt and freshly ground white pepper until the salt has dissolved.

Fold the prepared ingredients into 5 tablespoons olive oil. Salt and pepper to taste.

Combine 1 pinch each of salt and freshly ground white pepper, 1 tablespoon grated horseradish and 3 tablespoons pineapple juice with the grated apple.

Gently fold 4 tablespoons salad mayonnaise, 3 tablespoons ketchup, and 1 tablespoon white wine into the prepared ingredients with a whisk.

Important Techniques

Peeling Bell Peppers

Peppers of any hue give a salad freshness and color. They are most nutritious when eaten raw, but their skin is not easy to digest. Peel bell peppers when preparing food for people with sensitive stomachs.

1 Wash, dry and place the bell pepper on the roasting rack in an oven heated to 400°. Roast until the skin blisters.

2 Wrap the bell pepper in a damp cloth, let cool, and pull off skin with a sharp knife.

3 Quarter the bell pepper, remove all stems, ribs and seeds and then dice or cut into strips.

4 For bell pepper rings, halve the pepper horizontally. Remove all ribs and seeds and cut the halves into rings.

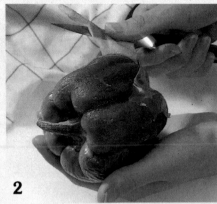
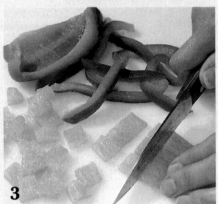

Chopping Onions

Never fight the tears of chopping onions again. Briefly put the onion, knife and cutting board under cold running water but do not dry. Master this technique for quickly dealing with onions, and there will be no crying.

1 Halve the peeled onion lengthwise. Make lengthwise incisions until just before the root end, but do not separate.

2 Holding the onion half together, make incisions parallel to the cutting board until just before the root end.

3 Cut the onion halves in thin slices; they will just come apart diced.

4 For onion rings, just slice the whole onion crosswise; the slices will come apart as rings.

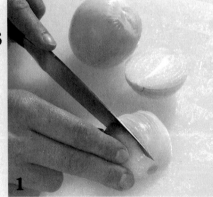

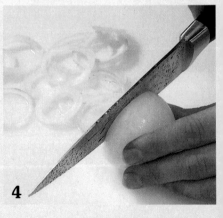

1

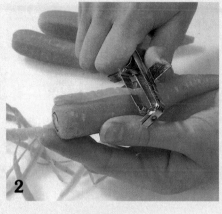

2

3

4

Cleaning Vegetables

Salads made of uncooked vegetables must be prepared with care. Besides the familiar salad vegetables, chicory, carrots, celery and zucchini are great raw, if you watch out for the following:

1 Remove the bad leaves from the outer chicory stalks, trim the root end and cut out the bitter wedge with a sharp knife.

2 Brush carrots well under running warm water, dry and peel with a knife or a vegetable-peeler, (grating loses too much juice).

3 Pull off the coarse fibers or strings from celery stalks and cut into strips or dice.

4 Dry washed zucchini, halve lengthwise, cut into strips lengthwise, and then cut the strips crosswise to get diced zucchini.

1

2

3

4

Chopping Herbs

Chop herbs shortly before use. If herbs sit around chopped for too long, they will lose a large part of their nutritional value. Herbs are usually weighed or chopped; occasionally, they will be cut into strips.

1 Thoroughly wash under running lukewarm water and dry herb bundles or sprigs.

2 Remove all coarse stems and lay the leaves onto the cutting board in bundles. Chop the leaves with a chopping knife.

3 Herbs can also be chopped with a broad, pointed knife. Holding the point, rock the edge back and forth over the herbs.

4 Chives should be dried right after washing and cut with a pair of kitchen scissors. Chives go straight into the dressing or the salad.

Appetizer Salads

Sophisticated and tasty salads always
make for a pleasant surprise, whether as an entree,
a between-meal snack, or a light meal.

Breast of Goose and Bell Pepper Salad

Somewhat expensive, quick

Preparation time: 25 minutes

1 red, 1 green, 1 yellow bell pepper
1 red chili pepper
2 shallots
1 clove garlic
¼ lb. mushrooms
1 tsp. butter
⅛ tsp. each salt and freshly ground black pepper
2 tbs. lemon juice
⅛ tsp. sugar
3 tbs. sesame oil
1 tbs. freshly chopped lemon balm
⅓ lb. smoked breast of goose, thinly sliced

Wash the bell peppers, remove stem, base of stem, ribs, and seeds. Cut the bell peppers into slender rings. • Rinse the chili pepper, halve, remove seeds and ribs, and cut the pepper in thin strips. • Peel and finely chop the shallots and garlic. • Clean, rinse and finely chop the mushrooms. • Melt the butter in a pan and sauté the shallots and garlic until translucent. Add the chopped mushrooms and simmer until the liquid is absorbed. Add 1 pinch each salt and pepper and allow to cool. • Combine the lemon juice, sugar, 1 pinch salt and pepper, stir in the oil, and add the mushroom mixture and the lemon balm. • Arrange the bell pepper rings on 4 plates, sprinkle the chili pepper strips over them, and place a portion of the mushroom marinade on each plate. Arrange the sliced breast of goose next to the marinade.

Field Salad with Pork Fillet

Somewhat expensive

Preparation time: 30 minutes

½ lb. wild greens
⅔ lb. pork fillet
2 oz. bacon
1 tsp. oil
2 pinches each salt and freshly ground black pepper
2 tbs. balsamic vinegar
1 tsp. medium mustard
6 tbs. nut oil

Rinse and dry the greens. • Skin the pork fillet. Dice the bacon. • Heat the oil in a pan and fry the bacon until crisp. Drain the bacon on a paper towel. • Sauté the pork fillet in the bacon fat for 10 minutes, sprinkle with salt and pepper, wrap in aluminum foil and put aside. • Blend the vinegar with mustard, a pinch each of salt and pepper and briskly stir in the oil. • Combine the greens with the marinade and put a portion on each plate. • Slice the fillet and arrange next to the salad. Dribble some marinade over the meat. • Sprinkle the bacon over the salad.

entil Salad with reast of Duck

kes a little longer

aking time: 2 hours
eparation time: 45 minutes

cup lentils
oz. bacon
small carrots
small onion
lb. wild greens
lb. breast of duck
pinches each salt and freshly
ound black pepper
tsp. marjoram
tbs. walnut oil
tbs. sherry vinegar

oak the lentils for 2 hours in
plenty of water, drain in a
ve, and cook about 15 min-
es in 1 quart water, but do not
them get too soft. Then drain
ell in a sieve. • Preheat the
en to 425°. • Dice the bacon.
eel the carrots and cut into
n slices. Peel and chop the
ion. Clean, rinse and dry the
ld greens. • Remove fat and
ndons from duck and rub in a
nch each of salt, pepper and
arjoram. • Heat 1 tablespoon
in a stew-pot and brown the
ck about 5 minutes, skin side
wn. Place the pot on the bot-
m rack of the oven, roast the
east of duck 10 minutes and
ke it out of the pot. • Fry
con in 1 tablespoon oil until
lden. Add the chopped onion
d carrot and allow to cook for
to 8 minutes. Prepare a sauce
m the vinegar, a pinch each of
t and pepper and 2 table-
oons oil. Combine with the
eens, and arrange on 4 plates.
range the lentils and bacon-
getable mixture (without the
oking oil) on the plates . •
ce the duck while still warm
d arrange shingle-like on the
til-vegetable mixture.

Shrimp-Pineapple Salad

Somewhat expensive, easy to prepare

Preparation time: 40 minutes
Marinating time: 15 minutes

¾ lb. small shrimp, cooked
4 slices pineapple
4 leaves lettuce
1 egg yolk
1 tsp. white wine vinegar
4 tbs. oil
1 tbs. pineapple juice
1 small ginger plum
1 shallot
1 pinch each salt and freshly ground white pepper
½ bunch parsley

Rinse and peel shrimp, drain, and pat dry. Peel the pineapple slices, cut into small wedges and remove the hard core. Save the juice. Combine with the shrimp. • Rinse and dry the lettuce leaves. •Blend the egg yolk with the vinegar, and add the oil bit by bit while stirring. Stir in the pineapple juice. • Finely chop the plums, peel and finely chop the shallot. Combine both with the sauce. Salt and pepper to taste. • Lay the salad leaves on 4 plates, spread the shrimp-pineapple mixture on each, and cover with the cocktail sauce. • Rinse and dry the parsley and garnish each plate with a sprig.

Shrimp-Asparagus Salad

Somewhat expensive, easy to prepare

Preparation time: 50 minutes

½ lb. medium-sized asparagus
2 cups water
1 pinch salt
1 pinch sugar
½ tsp. butter
4-6 leaves garden lettuce
1 egg yolk
½ tsp. mustard
5 tbs. sunflower oil
1 tbs. ketchup
1 tbs. cognac
⅛ tsp. each salt and freshly ground white pepper
A few dashes of angostura bitters
½ lb. small, peeled shrimp, cooked
A little watercress or dill

Peel the asparagus from top to bottom and cut off the woody bottom. Rinse in cold water and cut into 2 inch pieces • Add salt, sugar and butter to water and bring to a boil. Cook the asparagus in the simmering water for just 15 minutes and drain in a sieve. • Rinse and dry salad leaves and cut into thin strips. Arrange on 4 plates. • Blend the egg yolk with the mustard. Stir in the oil, at first drop by drop, then in a thin stream. Add the cognac and the ketchup and add salt, pepper and bitters to taste. • Combine the shrimp with the asparagus pieces, arrange on the plates and trickle dressing over them. • Garnish with dill or watercress.

Artichoke Cocktail

Somewhat expensive

Preparation time: 30 minutes

1 tbs. clarified butter
½ lb. boned chicken breast
2 egg yolks
1 pinch salt
1 tbs. lemon juice
½ cup oil
1 clove of garlic
6 tbs. ketchup
1 tbs. honey
1 pinch cayenne pepper
8 canned artichoke hearts
16 stuffed olives
¼ lb. cooked ham
1 bunch watercress
½ lemon

Heat the clarified butter in a pan. Brown the chicken at medium heat for 4 minutes to a side. Put aside chicken and let cool. • Blend the yolks, salt and lemon juice. Whisk in the oil at first drop by drop, then in a thin stream. • Peel and press the garlic into this mayonnaise. Add the ketchup, honey, cayenne and 2 to 3 tablespoons water. • Drain the artichoke hearts and olives. Quarter the artichokes. • Dice the ham, and slice the chicken. • Rinse and dry the garden cress. • Put half the mayonnaise on 4 plates. Arrange the artichoke, chicken, ham, olives and watercress on the plates. Pour the remaining mayonnaise over the plates and garnish with lemon slices.

Fruit on Iceberg Lettuce

Somewhat expensive, easy to prepare

Preparation time: 30 minutes

1 small head iceberg lettuce
1 tbs. herbal vinegar
1 pinch salt
2 tbs. seed oil
3 stalks celery
½ lb. strawberries
1 honeydew melon
1 avocado
½ lb. small, peeled shrimp, cooked
2 tbs. lemon juice
1 cup heavy cream
3 tbs. light mayonnaise
½ tsp. freshly ground white pepper
1 tbs. cognac
1 pinch sugar
1 sprig lemon balm

Separate the leaves from a head of iceberg lettuce, rinse and drain. Blend the vinegar with the salt and oil. Layer a bowl with the salad leaves and dribble the marinade over them. • Strip the coarse fibers from the celery stalks, rinse, pat dry and chop. • Rinse off strawberries, clean and halve; quarter the larger berries. • Halve the melon, clean out the seeds and scoop out the flesh in little balls. • Halve the avocado, remove the seed, peel and dice. • Rinse the shrimp under cold water and drain. Combine with the fruit and sprinkle the lemon juice over the mixture. • Whip the cream until it is half stiff. Combine with mayonnaise, pepper, cognac and sugar. • Heap the fruit salad on the iceberg lettuce and refrigerate. Pour the cream dressing over the salad and sprinkle the lemon balm on top.

Bell Pepper Salad with Salami

Inexpensive, quick

Preparation time: 20 minutes
Marinating time: 8 to 10 minutes

2 green bell peppers
1 red bell pepper
1 yellow bell pepper
1 large white onion
¼ lb. Hungarian salami, thinly sliced
½ handful parsley
2 cloves garlic
½ tsp. salt
3 tbs. red wine vinegar
2 tbs. seed oil
1 pinch freshly ground black pepper

Halve the bell peppers and remove seeds, ribs and stems. Rinse, dry and cut into thin strips. • Peel the onion and cut into slender rings. • Quarter the salami slices. • Combine the bell peppers, onion rings and salami in a bowl. • Rinse the parsley, pat dry, remove large stems, finely chop and sprinkle over salad. • Peel and chop the garlic, sprinkle the salt over the garlic, and crush. Blend with the red wine vinegar, oil, and peppers. Toss this marinade with the salad. Marinate the covered salad for 8 to 10 minutes. • Goes well with toasted whole-grain or fresh dark bread.

Tip: To make this salad a little fiery, take a small, but devilishly hot cherry pepper, remove all ribs and seeds, cut it into very thin strips, and add to the salad.

Radicchio and Cheese Salad

Inexpensive, easy to prepare

Preparation time: 30 minutes

1 large head radicchio
½ lb. mushrooms
2 red onions
⅓ lb. Emmenthaler cheese
1 pear
1 tsp. mustard
2 tbs. herbal vinegar
½ tsp. each salt and freshly ground black pepper
2 tbs. walnut oil
1 handful chives

Tear the radicchio into pieces, rinse and drain. • Clean, rinse, and drain the mushrooms. Thinly slice. • Peel the onions and cut into rings. Slice the Emmenthaler and cut into strips. • Rinse, quarter, remove seeds, peel and slice the pear. • Blend the mustard with the vinegar, salt and pepper. Blend in the oil and combine the dressing with the other ingredients. • Rinse, pat dry and chop the chives. Scatter them over the salad. • French bread accompanies this salad wonderfully.

Spinach Salad with Smoked Salmon

Somewhat expensive, quick

Preparation time: 30 minutes

½ lb. leaf spinach
1 large white onion
4 hard-boiled eggs
½ lb. smoked salmon
½ handful dill
2 tbs. lemon juice
pinch salt
pinch sugar
⅓ cup creamy yogurt
1 tbs. crème fraîche
2 tsp. coarsely ground black pepper

Pick out the bad leaves from the spinach, remove the coarser stems, rinse and drain well. • Peel the onion and cut into very thin rings. • Peel and slice the eggs. • Cut the salmon into strips. • Rinse, pat dry and chop the dill. • Lay the spinach on a salad platter or 4 plates. Spread the onion rings and salmon over the spinach and sprinkle the dill over the salad. Add the sliced egg. • Blend the lemon juice, salt and sugar. Also blend in the yogurt and crème fraîche; place a portion on each salad. Sprinkle the pepper over the salad.

Tip: Also shred the spinach and combine it with sliced egg, quartered tomatoes, onion rings, and use ham instead of salmon. Then just toss with a vinaigrette sauce (see "Favorite Dressings" section).

Green Bean Salad with Goose Liver Pâté

Somewhat expensive, easy to prepare

Preparation time: 30 minutes
Marinating time: 2 hours

1 lb. tender green beans
2 cups water
1 tsp. salt
4 sprigs summer savory
1 shallot
3 tbs. sherry vinegar
1 pinch each salt, freshly ground white pepper, and sugar
⅛ tsp. mustard
4 tbs. walnut oil
½ cup walnuts
⅓ lb. goose liver pâté flavored with truffles

Trim and rinse the beans. Put salt and 2 sprigs of summer savory in water and bring to a boil. Cook the beans for about 15 minutes. Remove and drain well. • Chop the remaining summer savory, peel and chop the shallot, and combine both with the vinegar, salt, pepper, sugar, and mustard. Blend in the walnut oil. • Add the beans and walnuts to the marinade and mix gently. Marinate for at least 2 hours. • Cut the pâté into thin slices and arrange alternately with the bean salad on plates. • Fresh white bread with salted butter accompanies this salad quite well.

Tip: If goose liver pâté is too expensive, substitute any other liver pâté.

Mussel Cocktail

Takes a little longer

Preparation time: 1 hour
Marinating time: 30 minutes

| 2 cloves garlic |
| 2 lbs. mussels |
| ½ cup dry white wine |
| Juice of 1 lemon |
| 1 pinch each salt and freshly ground white pepper |
| 6 tbs. olive oil |
| 2 tbs. chopped chives |
| ½ tsp. fresh marjoram leaves |
| ¾ lb. small mushrooms |
| 1 large lemon |

Peel and chop garlic. •
Thoroughly brush mussels under running water and clean, removing the "beard." Discard opened mussels. • Bring the mussels, garlic and wine to a boil and cook covered at high heat for about 10 minutes. By then all shells should have opened. Occasionally shake the pot vigorously. Pour the mussels into a sieve, discarding those that have not opened. Allow to cool and remove from shell. • Blend a salad dressing out of the lemon juice, salt, pepper and olive oil. Add the chives and marjoram. • Clean, rinse, and thinly slice the mushrooms. Combine with the mussels in a bowl. Pour the sauce over this mixture and toss gently. • Let stand for about 30 minutes • Cut the lemon into thin slices and lay out on a serving platter. Arrange the salad on these.

Asparagus and Ham on Millet Cakes

Nutritious recipe

Preparation time: 50 minutes

| ½ cup millet |
| 1 cup water |
| 1 pinch salt |
| ¼ cup milk |
| 1 lb. green asparagus |
| 2 eggs |
| ¼ cup cream |
| ½ tsp. each sea salt and curry |
| 1 tbs. butter |
| 1 tbs. chives |
| ¼ lb. smoked ham, lightly salted and cut into 8 slices |
| 2 tbs. white wine vinegar |
| 1 pinch sea salt |
| 1 or 2 pinches freshly ground white pepper |
| 2 tbs. safflower seed oil |
| 2 tbs. freshly chopped garden herbs: parsley, dill, tarragon, lemon balm |
| 1 hard-boiled egg |

Simmer the millet in the salted water for 15 minutes. Add milk and simmer another 5 minutes. Remove from heat and allow to swell for a further 10 minutes. • Rinse the asparagus, remove the woody ends, cook covered in water for 15 minutes and drain. • Blend the eggs, cream, salt and curry and combine with the millet. • Melt butter in pan and fry 4 small millet cakes. Place on 4 plates and scatter chives over the cakes. • Wrap the asparagus in the ham slices and arrange on plates. • Make a dressing of the vinegar, sea salt, pepper, oil and herbs. Peel and chop the egg and blend with the dressing. Serve the dressing separately.

Lobster Cocktail

Somewhat expensive, easy to prepare

Preparation time: 1 hour
Marinating time: 15 minutes

- lb. cauliflower florets
- lb. Kenya beans (or tender green beans)
- tsp. salt
- ripe banana
- juice of ½ lemon
- head of curly endive lettuce
- oz. canned lobster meat
- handful dill
- handful chives
- handful parsley
- tsp. tarragon mustard
- pinch freshly ground white pepper
- tbs. grape seed oil
- 3 tbs. dill vinegar
- pinch each salt and sugar

Briefly rinse the cauliflower and drain. Clean and rinse the beans. Cook each vegetable separately in lightly salted water for 8 to 10 minutes over low heat. Drain in a sieve. • Peel the banana and cut into even slices and sprinkle with lemon juice immediately. • Remove the leaves from the stem of the lettuce, tear into pieces, rinse and dry. Arrange on 4 plates. • Slice the lobster meat. • Arrange the cauliflower, beans, banana slices, and lobster on the plates. • Rinse and shake dry the dill, chives and parsley (save some dill for garnish) and finely chop. Blend with the tarragon mustard, pepper, oil, and dill vinegar. Salt and sugar to taste. Spoon dressing over salad. • Delicious with a baguette or buttered toast.

Avocado Platter with Shrimp

Somewhat expensive, quick

Preparation time: 20 minutes

| ¼ lb. fresh cheese |
| 6 tbs. sour cream |
| 16 shrimp, cooked |
| 2 ripe avocados |
| 2 tbs. lemon juice |
| 1 pinch salt |
| 1 pinch garlic pepper |
| Some lemon balm or dill for garnish |

Blend the cheese with the sour cream and spoon portions on 4 plates. • Peel and devein the shrimp, then rinse and pat dry. • Peel the skin off of the avocados, or, if they are not ripe enough for this, carefully cut off the skin. Halve lengthwise and take out the seed. Slice the fruit and arrange decoratively with the shrimp next to the sauce. Sprinkle both the shrimp and the avocado with lemon juice, salt and garlic pepper right away. • Rinse and dry the lemon balm or dill and garnish the salad. • Serve immediately, to avoid discoloration of the avocados.

Salad Platter with Quail Eggs

Somewhat expensive

Preparation time: 25 minutes

| 1 small head endive |
| ¼ lb. cherry tomatoes |
| 8 quail eggs (from a jar) |
| 2 tbs. sherry vinegar |
| 1 pinch each salt and freshly ground white pepper |
| 5 tbs. olive oil |
| ¾ lb. chanterelles mushrooms |
| 1 small clove garlic |
| Salt and pepper |

Separate the leaves of the endive, rinse and dry. Tear into pieces and distribute on 4 plates. • Rinse and halve the cherry tomatoes. Halve the quail eggs. Blend the sherry vinegar with 1 pinch each salt and pepper. Vigorously stir in 4 tablespoons olive oil. • Clean, rinse, drain and cut the mushrooms into strips. Peel the garlic clove. • Heat the remaining oil in a pan and add the mushrooms. Crush the garlic over the mushrooms and sauté them for about 8 minutes at medium heat. Then flavor with 1 pinch each salt and pepper. • Arrange the mushrooms, tomatoes and quail eggs on the salad and dribble the marinade over the salad. Serve immediately.

Tip: Substitute thinly sliced mushrooms for the chanterelles.

Chinese Cabbage with Oranges

Nutritious, easy to prepare

Preparation time: 15 minutes

⅓ lb. Chinese or Japanese cabbage (½ a small head)
⅓ cup raisins
1 orange
½ cup walnuts
⅓ cup cream
2 tbs. walnut oil
Juice of ½ lime
2 tbs. apple juice concentrate
½ cup cottage cheese
½ tsp. fresh or crumbled dried rosemary

Rinse the cabbage, drain well, and shred. • Rinse and drain the raisins. Peel the orange and remove the skin from the segments (put 4 aside for garnish). • Coarsely chop the nuts (put aside 4 halves for garnish). Combine all ingredients in a bowl. • Blend the cream, oil, lime juice, and apple juice concentrate and combine with the other ingredients. Add the cheese and the rosemary. Garnish with orange segments and nut halves.

Fruit Platter with Coconut

Nutritious, somewhat expensive

Preparation time: 20 minutes

1 medium carrot
⅓ cup raisins
Juice of ½ lime
1¼ cups fresh coconut (about ⅓ of a coconut)
8 fresh dates
1 mango
1 avocado
½ cup heavy cream
2 tsp. honey
1 pinch freshly ground white pepper
1 sprig lemon balm

Rinse, peel, and coarsely grate the carrot. Rinse and drain the raisins. Combine the grated carrot, raisins, and ½ tablespoon lime juice in a bowl. • Thinly slice the coconut. • Rinse, drain the dates, halve and remove the pits and stems. • Peel the mango, cut the meat from the seed and dice. • Peel and halve the avocado, remove the seed and cut the fruit into thin slices. • Arrange the prepared ingredients on 4 plates. Dribble ½ tablespoon lime juice over the avocado slices. • Whip the cream until half stiff and combine with the remaining lime juice, the honey and a little pepper. • Put a portion of the cream on each plate and garnish with lemon balm.

Radish and Ham Salad

Easy to prepare, quick

Preparation time: 20 minutes

2 white radishes
2 tbs. red wine vinegar
½ tsp. freshly ground white pepper
1 tsp. salt
1 tbs. walnut oil
⅓ lb. ham, lightly smoked and salted
1 handful chives

Peel, rinse, and slice the radishes, then cut into thin strips. • Combine the vinegar with the pepper and salt, then blend in the oil. Toss with the radishes. • Cut the ham into thin strips, removing the fatty edge, if necessary. Rinse, pat dry, and chop the chives. • Combine the ham and chives with the salad. Serve immediately. • Fresh dark bread and butter are quite tasty with this salad.

Tip: Since radishes lose their moisture pretty quickly, the salad should be prepared right before serving.

Carrots, grated and combined with the radishes, look very appetizing and lessen some of the radish's sharp flavor without making the salad lose piquancy.

Mixed Salad with Trout Fillet

Somewhat expensive, easy to prepare

Preparation time: 30 minutes

2 stalks chicory
¼ lb. wild greens
1 handful radishes
2 carrots, cooked
1 red bell pepper
4 smoked trout fillets
1 handful of mixed herbs: chervil, basil, and chives
1 handful watercress
3 tbs. herbal vinegar
½ tsp. salt
½ tsp. hot mustard
3 tbs. seed oil
2 hard-boiled eggs

Remove the root ends from the chicory stalks and cut out the bitter stem about 1 inch with a sharp knife. Cut the leaves into strips, rinse, and drain. •Discard any decayed leaves or tough stems, rinse, and drain or spin the wild greens. • Rinse, pat dry, and slice the radishes along with the carrots. • Halve the bell pepper, remove stem, ribs and seeds, rinse dry and dice. • Tear the trout fillets into pieces. • Rinse, pat dry and chop the herbs and the watercress. • Combine the vinegar with the salt and mustard, and blend in the oil. Add the herbs. • Toss all prepared ingredients lightly with the dressing. • Peel and chop the eggs and scatter over the salad.

Asparagus Salad with Sauce Béarnaise

Somewhat expensive

Preparation time: 45 minutes

| 2 shallots |
| 1 tbs. white wine vinegar |
| 1 cup white wine |
| 1 lb. each green and white asparagus |
| 1 tsp. salt |
| 1 pinch sugar |
| 1 tbs. lemon juice |
| ½ lb. firm tomatoes |
| ½ broiled chicken |
| ½ handful dill |
| 3 egg yolks |
| ⅔ cup butter |
| ⅛ tsp. each salt and cayenne pepper |

Peel the shallots, chop them and bring to a boil with the vinegar and white wine. Cook until about half done and let cool. • Peel the asparagus from top to bottom and cut off the woody part of stem. Tie the asparagus in bundles, cover with water. Add the salt, sugar, and lemon juice and bring to a boil; cook 15 to 20 minutes. • Peel, trim, remove the seeds from the tomatoes and dice. Bone the chicken and dice the meat. • Rinse, pat dry and chop the dill. • Cut off the tops of the asparagus in two inch pieces and halve. • Combine the diced tomato, asparagus, chicken and dill. • Whisk the egg yolks into the wine sauce. Melt the butter and blend it into the sauce in a thin stream. Add salt and cayenne to taste and then pour the dressing over the salad.

Chicken and Asparagus Salad

Requires some time

Preparation time: 1 hour
Marinating time: 30 minutes

1 chicken breast (about ½ lb.)
1 tsp. salt
4 peppercorns
1 small bay leaf
1 lb. medium asparagus
1 pinch sugar
1 tsp. butter
2 small tomatoes
4 pineapple slices
3 tbs. mayonnaise
3 tbs. sour cream
1 tbs. lemon juice
1 pinch each salt, sugar, and freshly ground white pepper
A dash of Worcestershire sauce
4 leaves Boston lettuce
1 bunch garden cress

Rinse the chicken and stew in 3 cups water with ½ teaspoon salt, peppercorns, and bay leaf for 20 minutes. Remove and let cool. • Meanwhile, peel and rinse the asparagus and cut into 2 inch pieces. Bring 2 cups water with ½ tsp salt, sugar and butter to a boil and cook the the asparagus for 15 to 20 minutes. Drain in a sieve. • Parboil the tomatoes, peel, quarter, remove the seeds and cut into strips. • Peel (if necessary) the pineapple slices and cut into small wedges. • Bone and dice the chicken. • Blend the mayonnaise with the sour cream, lemon juice, salt, pepper, sugar and Worcestershire sauce. Pour the dressing over the salad, toss gently, and marinate for 30 minutes. • Rinse the lettuce leaves and garden cress. Arrange the lettuce on 4 plates. Heap the salad on the leaves and garnish with the cress.

Asparagus and Eggs with Tuna Dressing

Quick, easy to prepare

Preparation time: 25 Minutes

4 eggs
24 asparagus stalks
1 tsp. salt
1 lump sugar
6½ oz. canned tuna
2 anchovy fillets
⅔ cup yogurt
1 tbs. lemon juice
1 tbs. capers
1 handful fresh dill
1 pinch freshly ground white pepper
4-8 leaves Boston lettuce

Pierce the round ends of the eggs (use a needle), cook them for 8 minutes, cool them under running water for a few seconds and peel. • Peel the asparagus and remove the woody end. Bring 2 cups water with the salt and sugar to a boil and cook the asparagus for about 15 minutes. Remove the asparagus, drain and let cool. • Drain the tuna and puree in a blender or chop together with the anchovies. Stir in the yogurt, lemon juice and capers. Rinse and shake the dill dry. Put aside the 4 nicest leaves for use as garnish. Remove the remaining leaves from the stems, cut into thin strips and combine with the sauce. Pepper to taste. • Rinse, dry and arrange the lettuce on 4 plates. • Halve or quarter the eggs and arrange with the asparagus and dressing. • This is particularly delicious with fresh French bread.

Egg-Mushroom Salad

Inexpensive, easy to prepare

Preparation time: 15 minutes

5 tbs. cream
2 tbs. sunflower seed oil
2 tbs. lemon juice
1 tsp. freshly grated horseradish
½ tsp. mustard
1 handful chives
½ handful parsley
1 pinch each salt, and freshly ground white pepper
1 pinch each sugar and freshly grated nutmeg
4 hard-boiled eggs
½ lb. mushrooms

Blend the cream, oil, lemon juice, horseradish and mustard to a creamy mixture. • Rinse and dry the parsley and chives. Chop the parsley and add to the dressing. Add salt, pepper, sugar and nutmeg to taste. • Peel and slice the eggs. • Clean, rinse and thinly slice the mushrooms. • Arrange the egg and mushroom slices on 4 plates and put some dressing over them. • Chop the chives and sprinkle over the servings. Toast or a baguette accompany this salad quite well.

Shrimp on Field Salad

Somewhat expensive

Preparation time: 45 minutes

½ lb. wild greens
½ honeydew melon
1 small zucchini
3 tbs. vinegar
2 pinches each salt and freshly ground white pepper
½ tsp. Dijon mustard
½ tsp. finely chopped capers
2 tbs. freshly chopped herbs: parsley, basil, borage, pimpernel
4 tbs. olive oil
1 lemon
8 shrimp
1 tsp. salt
2 cloves garlic
2 tbs. butter
2 tbs. freshly chopped parsley
4 sprigs lemon balm

Pick over, rinse and dry the wild greens. • Halve the melon, remove the seeds and make melon balls of the flesh. Rinse the zucchini, cut off the ends and slice the vegetable. • Blend the vinegar, 1 pinch salt and 1 pinch pepper, the mustard, capers, herbs and oil. • Slice the lemon and cook in plenty of salted water with the shrimp for about 8 minutes. Remove the shrimp, let cool and shell. • Peel and chop the garlic. Melt the butter in a large saucepan, sauté the garlic, parsley and shrimp 2 to 3 minutes. Add a pinch of salt and pepper. • Combine the field salad, melon balls, and zucchini slices with the dressing and arrange on 4 plates. Put 2 shrimp on each plate and garnish with lemon balm.

Figaro Salad

Easy to prepare, quick

Preparation time: 30 minutes

2 medium-sized red beets
2 bunches celery
¼ lb. pickled tongue
1 small head Boston lettuce
2 tbs. mayonnaise
4 finely chopped anchovy fillets
2 tbs. ketchup
1 tbs. red wine vinegar
1 pinch each salt, sugar, and freshly ground white pepper

Thoroughly brush the beets under running water, peel, and cut into matchstick-sized strips. • Rinse the celery. Cut off the root ends and the leaf stems. Pull off the tough fibers as with rhubarb. Then slice the celery into pieces about ¼ inch thick. • Slice the pickled tongue into similarly thin pieces. • Liberally remove the outer leaves from the lettuce. Rinse the "heart" thoroughly, dry and shred. Combine the salad ingredients. • Blend the mayonnaise, anchovies, ketchup, red wine vinegar, salt, pepper, sugar and add a little water or milk in order to make the dressing more liquid. Add spices to taste for the sweet-and-sour effect. • Lightly toss the marinade with the salad.

Matjes Salad with Cucumber

Easy to prepare, inexpensive

Preparation time: 20 minutes

pickled white (Matjes) herring fillets
tbs. heavy cream
tbs. yogurt
tbs. lemon juice
½ small onion
handful each of parsley, dill, and chives
pinch each salt, sugar, and freshly ground black pepper
½ cucumber
bunch radishes
leaves Boston lettuce
lemon wedges

Soak the herring, (the amount of water needed will depend on how salted they are), and put in a cool place. • Whip the cream and blend with the yogurt and lemon juice. • Peel the onion and crush or grate into the yogurt-cream. • Rinse and dry the dill, parsley and chives. Put aside some of the herbs for use as garnish, chop the remainder. Combine these herbs with the dressing, then add sugar, salt and pepper to taste. • Peel the cucumber, halve lengthwise, and remove the seeds with a spoon. Thinly slice the cucumber. • Trim and rinse the radishes, and cut them into thin slices. • Rinse, dry and arrange the salad leaves on four shallow bowls. • Pat the herring dry and cut into thin strips. • Pour about ⅓ of the dressing into the bowls. Arrange the herring pieces, radishes and cucumber on the dressing. Then apportion the remaining dressing. • Garnish with the reserved herbs and the lemon wedges. • Whole-kernel breads with butter fit this dish perfectly.

Cucumber Salad with Shrimp

Easy to prepare, somewhat expensive

Preparation time: 30 minutes

2 eggs
1 cucumber
1 tsp. salt
2 tbs. white wine vinegar
2 tbs. soy sauce
½ tsp. sugar
3 tbs. sunflower seed oil
½ lb. cooked shrimp
1 handful dill

Pierce the eggs at the larger end with a needle, lay into boiling water and cook for about 8 minutes. Rinse briefly with cold water, peel, and allow to cool. • Vigorously rub the cucumber with a kitchen towel, then rinse it in lukewarm water, dry and halve. Spoon out the seeds and then dice the cucumber into ¼ inch pieces. • Blend the salt, white wine vinegar, soy sauce and sugar, until the salt and sugar have dissolved. Whisk the sunflower seed oil into this dressing and toss with the shrimp and cucumber. • Wash, dry and remove the stems from the dill, then chop. • Arrange the salad in a bowl and sprinkle the dill over it. • Slice each egg into 8 wedges and decorate the salad with them. • Fresh baked bread or rolls are delicious with this salad.

Oak Leaf Salad with Salmon

Somewhat expensive, easy to prepare

Preparation time: 45 minutes

1 small head oak leaf lettuce
⅔ lb. small mushrooms
2 tbs. lemon juice
2 shallots
2 to 3 tbs. balsamic vinegar
1 pinch each salt and freshly ground black pepper
½ tsp. dried tarragon
4 tbs. olive oil
½ lb. smoked salmon
1 tbs. coarsely chopped parsley

Discard any decayed leaves and remove tough stems from lettuce, wash and drain or dry. Halve or quarter the larger leaves. • Clean, rinse and thinly slice the mushrooms. Dribble the lemon juice over the mushroom slices in order to keep them from discoloring. • Peel and chop the shallots. • Blend the balsamic vinegar, salt, pepper, tarragon, shallots and olive oil. • Draw the lettuce through the marinade and arrange on four plates. Then marinate the mushrooms in the dressing briefly and arrange them on the plates as well. • Finally, cut the salmon into 8 evenly sized slices and put two slices on each plate. • Garnish with the parsley and serve with French bread and salted butter.

Cauliflower and Cheese Salad

Nutritious, easy to prepare

Preparation time: 25 minutes

1 lb. cauliflower florets
½ lb. zucchini
⅓ lb. each of mozzarella and mild cheddar cheese
⅓ cup cream
1 tbs. each of walnut oil and maple syrup
2 tbs. lemon juice
1 tsp. red peppercorns
1 tbs. unblanched almonds
1 sprig lemon balm

Rinse the cauliflower, halve the larger florets. Steam for about 10 minutes (should still be firm and crisp) and let drain and cool in a sieve. • Rinse and trim the zucchini and dice. • Dice the cheese. • Blend the cream with oil, maple syrup, and lemon juice. Crush the peppercorns and combine with sauce. • Combine the drained cauliflower, the diced zucchini and the cheese in a bowl. Pour the sauce over them and toss well. Strew the coarsely grated almonds over the salad. Serve on plates garnished with lemon balm.

Tip: If desired salt the salad, use sea salt, but add it only at the end.

Cheese Salad with Nuts

Easy to prepare, quick

Preparation time: 30 minutes

1 lb. yogurt
4 tbs. lemon juice
1 tbs. freshly grated horseradish
2 tsp. sugar
1 pinch salt
½ cup heavy cream
½ cup walnuts
½ cup hazelnuts
¼ lb. Camembert cheese (not too soft)
¼ lb. fresh Gouda cheese
1 celery stalk
1 large red apple
1 head endive or Batavian lettuce

Blend the yogurt, lemon juice, horseradish, sugar and salt. Whip the cream and blend it into the dressing as well. • Put aside some of the walnuts for garnish. Coarsely chop the remainder. Chop the hazelnuts somewhat more finely. Combine the nuts with the dressing. • Cut the cheeses into strips (remember to take the rind off of the Gouda). • Take the more tender inner stalk of celery and rinse and slice it. Save the outer stalks for soup. • Rinse and quarter the apple, remove the seed housing. First slice the quarters, then cut into strips. • Combine the cheese, celery, and apple with the dressing. • Rinse and dry the lettuce. Cut the lettuce into small pieces and spread on the serving plates. • Arrange the cheese salad on the lettuce and garnish with the reserved walnuts.

Tofu-Mango Salad

Nutritious

Preparation time: 40 minutes

1 lb. tofu
2 tbs. unpeeled sesame seeds
1 small head oak leaf lettuce
1 large ripe mango (about 14 oz.)
2 tbs. soy sauce
¼ tsp. freshly ground black pepper
3 tbs. sesame seed oil
2 tbs. lemon juice
½ cup heavy cream or crème fraîche
1-2 tsp. freshly grated ginger
2 tsp. honey
1 tbs. chopped chives

Cut the tofu into thick slices, lay it onto a clean, folded kitchen towel, cover with the towel, and use a board and some weights to press out some moisture for about 15 minutes. • Roast the sesame seeds in a pan over medium heat, turning frequently. • Pick out the nice leaves from the lettuce, rinse, and dry. • Peel the mango and thinly slice the flesh. • Dribble 1 tablespoon soy sauce over the pressed tofu and sprinkle with half the pepper. • Heat 1 tablespoon sesame seed oil in a skillet and sauté the tofu slices for about 5 minutes, spiced side down. Dribble 1 tablespoon soy sauce over the tofu slices and sprinkle with remaining pepper. Turn the tofu slices and sauté another 5 minutes. • Toss the lettuce in a large bowl with 1 tablespoon each oil and lemon juice and then arrange in a serving bowl. • Make a dressing with the heavy cream, 1 tablespoon oil, 1 tablespoon lemon juice, the ginger, honey and chives, and pour over lettuce. Lay the mango slices on this salad. Sprinkle half of the sesame seeds over the salad. Cube the tofu, arrange with the rest of the salad, and sprinkle the remaining sesame seeds over the salad.

Oak Leaf Lettuce with Cheese Croutons

Inexpensive, quick

Preparation time: 20 minutes

head oak leaf lettuce	
day-old roll	
cloves garlic	
tbs. cold pressed olive oil	
tbs. freshly grated pecorino or Parmesan cheese	
tbs. herbal vinegar	
½ tsp. salt	
pinch freshly ground black pepper	

Pick out decayed leaves and tough stems from the lettuce, cut it into strips, rinse and drain. • Cut the roll into ½ inch slices, then make cubes of the slices. • Peel and press the garlic into the olive oil. • Heat 1 tablespoon olive oil in a pan and brown the bread cubes until they are golden. Sprinkle the grated cheese over them and continue browning until the cheese melts. • Blend the salt and pepper into the vinegar, add 4 tablespoons oil and toss with the lettuce. • Serve the salad with the croutons strewn over the oak leaf lettuce.

<u>Tip</u>: If oak leaf lettuce is unavailable substitute any other leafy lettuce: field lettuce, curly endive, Boston, or regular endive.

Buckwheat Salad

Nutritious, inexpensive

Preparation time: 40 minutes

1 qt. water	
½ tsp. salt	
½ tsp. thyme dried and crumbled	
1 small bay leaf	
2 tbs. sunflower seed oil	
½ cup buckwheat	
3 tomatoes	
3 shallots	
1 oz. anchovy fillets	
⅔ cup sour cream	
1 tbs. lemon juice	
1 pinch freshly ground black pepper	
2 tbs. chopped chives	

Bring the water with the salt, thyme, bay leaf and 1 tablespoon oil to a boil, pour in the buckwheat kernels and simmer uncovered for 15 minutes. Take the pot off the heat and let sit for another 5 minutes while the kernels swell. Drain in a sieve and allow to cool then take out the bay leaf. • While the wheat is cooking, parboil the tomatoes, rinse, peel and cut them in thin slices. • Peel the shallots, make thin rings of 2 shallots and finely chop the third. • Finely chop ⅓ of the anchovies, halve the remainder lengthwise. • Make a dressing by blending the sour cream, 1 tablespoon oil, the lemon juice, pepper, the chopped ingredients and ½ of the chives. Combine about ⅔ of the dressing with the buckwheat. • Heap the buckwheat salad in a ring of tomato slices and onion (shallot) rings, arrange the anchovies on this salad, pour the remaining dressing over the middle of the salad and sprinkle with the chives.

Spinach Salad with Feta Cheese

Nutritious, quick

Preparation time: 25 minutes

½ lb. leaf spinach
⅓ lb. feta cheese
2 tbs. olive oil
2 tbs. cream
2 tbs. lemon juice
⅔ cup blanched almonds
10 black olives
2 shallots
1 pinch freshly ground black pepper

Rinse the spinach and pick out the decayed leaves and tough stems, drain and cut into thin strips. • Using a fork, blend the oil, cream, and lemon juice into about ½ of the cheese. • Roast the almonds in a dry, heavy skillet or saucepan, until they get a little color and just start to have a nice aroma. Pit the olives and finely chop. Peel the shallots and slice to make thin rings. Thinly slice the remaining cheese. Combine the prepared ingredients with the spinach and pepper to taste. Serve the dressing separately.

Tip: Replace the almonds with pine nuts or roasted sunflower seeds.

Spinach and Egg Salad

Nutritious, inexpensive

Preparation time: 20 minutes

¼ lb. spinach
¼ lb. dandelion greens
1 box garden cress
3½ oz. cream cheese
1 cup yogurt
1 tbs. sunflower seed oil
1 tbs. lemon juice
1 tsp. salt
2 tsp. mustard
1 pinch freshly ground black pepper
2 shallots
3 hard-boiled eggs

Rinse the spinach and dandelion greens and pick out the decayed leaves. Pick out the tough stems from the spinach, dry and cut the leaves in thin strips. • Cut the cress from the roots, rinse, and drain. • Blend the yogurt with the cream cheese (using a fork) until sauce is creamy. Blend in the oil, lemon juice, salt, mustard, and pepper. • Peel the shallots and slice into thin rings, then combine with the other salad ingredients. Arrange the salad on 4 plates. • Peel, coarsely chop and sprinkle the eggs over the salad. Serve the dressing separately.

Tip: To use wild dandelion for this salad, only use very young and tender leaves, otherwise the salad will become too bitter.

Cucumber-Shrimp Cocktail

Nutritious

Preparation time: 20 minutes

small stalks Belgian endive	
small cucumber (about ¾ lb.)	
seedless orange	
ripe pears	
tbs. freshly squeezed lime juice	
½ tsp. sea salt	
pinch freshly ground white pepper	
½ cup heavy cream or crème fraîche	
tbs. walnut oil	
tbs. maple syrup	
½ tsp. mustard	
½ cup walnuts	
⅓ lb. small shrimp, cooked	
tbs. fresh dill	
sprigs dill	

Cut off the root ends of the endive and make a wedge-shaped cut to remove the bitter end of the stalk. Separate the leaves, rinse and drain. • Peel and dice the cucumber. • Peel the orange and remove the white rind, peel the segments and cut these into small slices. • Rinse, dry, and quarter the pears, core and dice the fruit. • Blend the lime juice, salt and pepper, then blend in the heavy cream, walnut oil, mustard, and maple syrup. • Put the cucumber cubes, orange pieces, and diced pear in a bowl with the walnuts, shrimp and dill and toss with the dressing. Stand the endive leaves in 4 cocktail bowls, fill with salad, and garnish with the sprigs of dill.

Fennel Salad with Turkey Breast

Somewhat expensive, easy to prepare

Preparation time: 30 minutes
Marinating time: 15 minutes

1 cup crème fraîche	
1 egg yolk	
1 tbs. freshly grated Parmesan cheese	
2 tbs. lemon juice	
1 pinch each salt and freshly ground white pepper	
1 pinch each sugar and cinnamon	
1 orange	
1 apple	
2 spring onions	
⅔ cup fresh dates	
½ lb. sliced turkey breast	
2 fennel bulbs	

Blend the crème fraîche with the egg yolk, Parmesan and lemon juice. Add salt, pepper, sugar and cinnamon to taste. • Peel the orange, and then peel the segments, saving the juice. Cut into sections and add to the dressing. • Rinse and quarter the apple, then remove the seed housing. Slice the quarters and add to the dressing immediately. • Use only the white and light green parts of the spring onions. Rinse and slice into fine rings. • Pit the dates. • Cut the turkey slices into strips. • Put the tender greens of the fennel aside. Rinse and cut the fennel into thin strips. • Toss the fennel, onions, dates and turkey with the dressing. • Let the salad marinate for 15 minutes, then sprinkle the chopped fennel greens over it.

Zucchini Salad with Black Olives

Easy to prepare, inexpensive

Cooling time: 3 hours
Preparation time: 25 minutes

1¼ lbs. small zucchini
Some ice cubes
1 firm tomato
1 white onion
3 tbs. lemon juice
1 pinch each salt and freshly ground white pepper
5 tbs. olive oil
3 sprigs mint
5-6 rosemary needles
12 black olives
2 oz. mozzarella cheese

Rinse and trim the zucchini. Place the zucchini in a bowl with the ice cubes and some water and put in the refrigerator for 3 hours. • Rinse, dry, and cut the tomato into eighths, removing the stem. • Peel, halve and slice the onion. • Make a dressing with the lemon juice, salt, pepper, and olive oil, blending thoroughly with a whisk. • Rinse the mint and pick the leaves. Put aside a few for use as garnish. Cut the rest into thin strips and add to the dressing with finely chopped rosemary needles. • Thinly slice the cooled and dried zucchini. Combine the zucchini, tomato, onion, and black olives in a bowl and toss with the dressing. • Dice the mozzarella and sprinkle over the salad. Garnish with mint.

Celery-Endive Salad

Easy to prepare, inexpensive

Preparation time: 30 minutes

1 lb. celery
½ head endive lettuce
3 tbs. wine vinegar
1 pinch each salt and freshly ground black pepper
1 tsp. mustard
4 tbs. olive oil
2 tbs. mayonnaise
¼ lb. cooked ham
1 sour apple
3½ oz. canned mushrooms

Cut the celery apart at the root end, so that the stalks fall apart. Separate the tender celery leaves, rinse and cut into fine strips. Rinse, dry and cut the celery stalks in ½ inch pieces. • Take off the outer green leaves from the endive, separate the tender yellow leaves and rinse under lukewarm water. Dry the leaves and shred. • Thoroughly blend the vinegar, salt, pepper, mustard and olive oil, then mix with the mayonnaise. • Dice the ham. Peel and quarter the apple then remove the seed housing. Cube the quarters. • Combine the celery pieces, endive, drained mushrooms, ham, and cubed apple in a bowl. Pour the salad dressing over these and toss well. Strew the celery leaves over the salad. • Serve well chilled.

Orange-Celery Salad

Easy to prepare, inexpensive

Preparation time: 30 minutes

3 oranges	
2 sour apples	
2 tbs. lemon juice	
1/4 celeriac	
1 egg yolk	
1/2 tsp. Dijon mustard	
4 tbs. safflower seed oil	
2 pinches each salt and freshly ground white pepper	
4 sprigs mint	

Peel the oranges and apples. Take apart the orange segments and slice. • Rinse the apples, rub dry, halve and remove the seed housing. Cut the apple halves into thin strips and dribble 1 tablespoon lemon juice over them immediately. • Peel and grate the celeriac and marinate with 1 tablespoon lemon juice. • Blend the egg yolk with the mustard. Blend in the safflower seed oil, at first drop by drop, then in a thin stream, constantly stirring with a whisk. Salt and pepper to taste. • Loosely combine the orange pieces, apple and celeriac in a bowl. Pour the dressing over this and gently toss. • Rinse and separate the mint leaves, leave a few whole, and cut the rest into thin strips. Toss these strips with the salad. Arrange the salad in 4 salad bowls, serve chilled and garnished with mint leaves.

Caruso Salad

Easy to prepare, famous recipe

Preparation time: 30 minutes

4 slices fresh pineapple	
2 medium-sized ripe tomatoes	
8 leaves Boston lettuce	
6 tbs. sour cream	
1-2 tsp. lemon juice	
1 tsp. honey	
1 pinch salt	
1 pinch ground cloves	
2 sage leaves	

Peel the pineapple slices and take out the hard core. Then dice the pineapple. • Make a crosswise incision on the stemless end of the tomatoes, parboil, and peel off the loosened skin. Then dice the tomatoes, removing the stem. • Rinse the lettuce leaves under lukewarm water, dry and arrange in 4 cocktail glasses. • Blend the sour cream with the lemon juice, honey, salt and ground cloves to taste. Combine this dressing with the pineapple and tomato pieces, spice to taste again and fill the cocktail glasses with the salad.• Rinse the sage in lukewarm water, dry and cut into thin strips. Sprinkle these over the salad portions. • Crackers with horseradish butter accompany this wonderfully.

Artichoke Hearts with Scampi

Quick, easy to prepare

Preparation time: 20 minutes

2 shallots
3 hard-boiled eggs
3 tbs. wine vinegar
2 pinches each salt and freshly ground white pepper
2 pinches sugar
2 tsp. small capers
1 tbs. freshly chopped herbs: chervil, parsley, dill, tarragon, pimpernel
½ tsp. Dijon mustard
6 tbs. olive oil
1 lb. cooked and peeled scampi (shrimp)
8 canned artichoke hearts
1 lime
4 sprigs dill

Peel and chop the shallots. • Peel and dice the hard-boiled eggs. • Blend the vinegar, salt, pepper, sugar, capers, herbs, mustard and chopped shallots. Add the olive oil and eggs. • Rinse and dry the scampi. • Drain the artichoke hearts and fill with the dressing. Arrange these with the scampi on plates. • Thinly slice the lime and use with the dill as garnish.

Chicken Fillets on Orange Slices

Easy to prepare, takes some time

Preparation time: 40 minutes
Marinating time: 1 hour

¾ lb. boned chicken breast
2 tsp. flour
1-2 tbs. butter
5 oranges
1 tsp. salt
2 pinches freshly ground white pepper
1 tbs. dried tarragon
2 medium-sized stalks chicory
2 shallots
4 tbs. crème fraîche
4 tbs. tarragon mustard

Rinse the chicken under cold water, pat dry, and cut into ¾ inch cubes. Dredge the chicken through the flour. • Melt the butter in a saucepan, and sauté the meat for about 10 minutes. • Press out the juice of 2 oranges and pour over the meat. Spice the meat with ½ teaspoon salt, 1 pinch pepper, and the tarragon. Marinate, covered, for at least an hour. Stir occasionally. • Remove the outer bad leaves from the chicory, remove the root part and cut out the bitter wedge at the base. Rinse the chicory stalks and slice into roughly ½ inch rings. • Peel the remaining oranges like apples, so that the white rind is also removed. Thinly slice the oranges, arrange on plates. Apportion the chicory rings and chicken in the middle of each plate. • Peel and finely chop the shallots and combine with the crème fraîche, mustard, a pinch of salt and a pinch of pepper into a dressing. Spoon the dressing over the chicory rings and chicken.

Large Vegetable Platter

Easy to prepare

Preparation time: 45 minutes

small white radish
medium carrot
yellow bell pepper
¼ lb. sauerkraut
small onion
A few leaves of chicory or endive
box garden cress
tbs. wheat sprouts
tbs. apple vinegar
tbs. cottage cheese
tsp. maple syrup
½ tsp. salt
pinch freshly ground white pepper
pinch paprika powder

Thinly peel and coarsely grate the radish. • Peel, rinse and likewise grate the carrot. • Halve the bell pepper, remove the stem, ribs and seeds, rinse the halves, dry and cut into thin strips. Halve the strips of pepper. Arrange the pepper strips, sauerkraut and grated vegetables on a platter. • Peel and chop the onion. • Rinse and dry the chicory or endive, remove the decayed or bad leaves and cut the remaining leaves into strips. Combine with the onion and arrange on the platter as well. • Cut the cress, rinse and drain. • Rinse the sprouts under lukewarm water, drain and arrange on the platter. • Whisk the vinegar together with the cottage cheese, maple syrup, salt, pepper, and paprika powder until creamy. Spice the dressing to taste and dribble a little over each salad. Scatter the cress over the platter.

Sicilian Shallots

Takes some time

Preparation time: 40 minutes

1½ lbs. shallots
1 tsp. salt
6 tbs. olive oil
1 tsp. sugar
⅓ cup mild wine vinegar
1 pinch each salt and freshly ground white pepper

Peel the shallots and then boil for about 10 minutes in salted water; they should still be a bit crisp. Drain in a sieve. • Heat the oil in a flat frying pan. Lay the shallots into the pan in one layer and sauté on all sides. Sprinkle the sugar over the shallots and continue cooking for another 4 to 5 minutes, turning the shallots carefully. Pour in the vinegar and add salt and pepper. • Let cool and serve as appetizer or side dish with cold meat or smoked fish.

Tip: Prepare this delicious vegetable ahead of time. Put the shallots (cooked and with the vinegar) into jars with screwtop lids while they are still hot and shut the jars right away. They will keep in the refrigerator for several days. (If shallots are unavailable, use onions, but slice or quarter the larger ones.) To make salad even more attractive add 1 red and 1 green pepper. Remove all stems, ribs, and seeds, rinse and cut into strips. Blanch very briefly (about 3 min.) in a little salted water, drain, and sauté with the onions or shallots.

Marinated Eggplant

Easy to prepare, inexpensive

Preparation time: 45 minutes
Marinating time: 24 hours

½ lbs. eggplant
tbs. salt
or 3 cloves garlic
tsp. oregano
tbs. olive oil
cup white wine vinegar
cup dry white wine
tsp. each salt and cayenne pepper

Rinse the eggplant and cut off the stems. Cut into ¼ inch thick slices, sprinkle the salt over the slices and set aside for 30 minutes. • Peel the garlic and chop together with the oregano.

• Rinse the eggplant slices, press and pat dry with paper towels. Sauté the eggplant bit by bit in the heated olive oil until golden brown, then drain on paper towels. • Make a marinade of the vinegar, wine, garlic and oregano, cayenne and salt; pour it over the eggplant and marinate for 24 hours.

Marinated Carrots

Inexpensive, easy to prepare

Preparation time: 30 minutes
Marinating time: 24 hours

1 lb. young, medium carrots
½ tsp. salt
3 cloves garlic
4 tbs. wine vinegar

1 pinch salt
1 pinch cayenne pepper
5 tbs. olive oil
½ tsp. fresh or 1 pinch dried oregano

Remove the root ends and the leaf stems from the carrots. Brush the carrots under running water and then cook for 20 minutes in salted water. Drain in a sieve and then quarter lengthwise. Cut these quarters into 1 to 1½ inch pieces. • Peel and chop the garlic cloves. • Blend a marinade of the garlic, vinegar, salt, cayenne pepper, olive oil and oregano and mix well with the carrots. • Marinate for 24 hours.

Marinated Fennel

Easy to prepare

Preparation time: 1 hour

4 fennel bulbs (about 1½ lb.)
1 tsp. salt
1 handful parsley
4 tbs. lemon juice
2 pinches white pepper

Remove the stems, root part, and harder outer ribs from the fennel. Rinse the bulbs and cook in salted water for 40 minutes, then drain. • Rinse, dry and chop the parsley. • Cut the fennel bulbs lengthwise into 4 to 6 pieces, put these in a bowl, and sprinkle the lemon juice and parsley over them. Spice with the freshly ground pepper.

Favorite Side Dish Salads

The time of the lonely lettuce leaf
is past. There are plenty of impressive
alternatives—nowadays a fine side dish
can even become the main attraction.

Tomato Salad

Quick, easy to prepare

Preparation time: 20 minutes

1 lb. small ripe tomatoes
3 shallots
½ tsp. salt
4 pinches freshly ground black pepper
1 tbs. white wine vinegar
1 tsp. lemon juice
3 tbs. olive oil
½ handful thyme

Wipe the tomatoes with a kitchen towel, rinse them in lukewarm water, then dry. Slice the tomatoes and remove the woody stem end. Arrange the slices on a platter. • Peel and chop the shallots. Sprinkle the chopped shallots over the tomatoes. • Evenly sprinkle the salt and pepper over the tomatoes. • Blend the white wine vinegar with the lemon juice and olive oil and dribble the dressing over the salad. • Rinse the thyme under lukewarm water, dry, remove tough stems and decayed leaves, and then chop the thyme. Sprinkle over the salad just before serving. • Depending on the main course, German black bread goes well with this dish.

Tip: If large tomatoes are preferred, then it would be best to cut them into 1 inch cubes. Reserve the juice and seeds and use them in the dressing, since they contain valuable nutrients.

Four Season Salad

Easy to prepare, quick

Preparation time: 30 minutes

2 medium tomatoes
1 small shallot
½ cucumber
1 large bunch radishes
1 small head Boston lettuce (or endive)
1 box garden cress
1 to 2 tbs. (fruit-based) vinegar
1 pinch each freshly ground white pepper and sugar
½ tsp. salt
3 tbs. sunflower seed oil
1 slice white bread

Rinse the tomatoes under lukewarm water, dry and cut each into 8 wedges. Remove the woody parts. Arrange the tomatoes on a platter and sprinkle with salt. • Peel and chop the shallots, then sprinkle over the tomatoes. • Rinse the cucumber under lukewarm water, rub dry, and cut into ¼ inch thick sticks. • Trim the radishes, rinse, dry and slice. • Remove the decayed leaves from the head of lettuce, rinse the inner leaves. Dry the head of lettuce, quarter and cut into wide strips. • Arrange each vegetable on the platter. • Cut the cress from its bed, rinse and drain. • Blend the vinegar, salt, pepper, and sugar. Add 2 tablespoons sunflower seed oil and dribble the dressing over all salad ingredients. • Dice the white bread and sauté in 1 tablespoon oil until all sides are crispy. • Sprinkle the cress and croutons over the salad.

Fennel Salad

Easy to prepare, quick

Preparation time: 30 minutes

1 tbs. white wine vinegar	
1/2 tsp. mustard	
1 pinch cayenne pepper	
4 tbs. walnut oil	
1 red apple	
2 oranges	
2 fennel bulbs (about 1 lb.)	
1 pinch salt	
8 walnut halves	

Blend the vinegar, mustard, cayenne and oil to make a thick marinade. • Rinse and quarter the apple, then core. • Slice the apple quarters and combine with the marinade. • Peel the oranges like apples, so that the white rind is also removed. Skin the segments and reserve any juice for the marinade. Combine the orange pieces with the apples. • Pick off the tender greens from the fennel, rinse and reserve. Trim away the tough stems, woody outer leaves and the root end. Rinse the bulbs, halve and slice very thinly. Sprinkle the fennel with the salt, combine with the fruit and marinade. Allow to marinate covered for about 5 minutes. • Meanwhile, coarsely chop the walnuts and chop the fennel greens. Sprinkle the fennel greens and walnuts over the salad and serve right away.

Celery-Walnut Salad

Easy to prepare, quick

Preparation time: 20 minutes

1 lb. celery	
1 large sour apple	
3 tbs. lemon juice	
1 pinch each salt, sugar and freshly ground white pepper	
4 tbs. sunflower seed oil	
3/4 cup walnuts	

Rinse, trim and remove the tough fibers from the celery. Slice the stalks into 1/2 inch pieces. • Peel and quarter the apple, then core. Cut the apple quarters into pieces about the same size as the celery. • Whisk together the lemon juice, salt, pepper, sugar and oil and pour the dressing over the celery and apple pieces. Toss well. • Quarter the walnuts and add to the salad. • Sprinkle the chopped celery leaves over the salad, which tastes best when served with lightly toasted dark bread.

Tip: For this salad to be particularly sophisticated, replace the sunflower seed oil with walnut oil. This oil is also well-suited to other salads that include nuts.

Chicory Salad with Mushrooms

Easy to prepare, quick

Preparation time: 20 minutes

1 clove garlic
2 tbs. red wine vinegar
1 tbs. soy sauce
1 tsp. mustard
1 pinch sugar
5 tbs. sunflower seed oil
1 lb. chicory
¼ lb. mushrooms
1 bell pepper (yellow or red)
1 tbs. freshly chopped parsley

Halve the garlic clove and rub the inside of the salad bowl with it. • Blend the vinegar, soy sauce, mustard, and sugar in the bowl. Vigorously blend in the oil so that a thick marinade is made. • Cut off the root ends of the chicory and make a wedge-shaped incision to remove the bitter end of the stem. Rinse the chicory leaves, dry or drain well. • Clean, rinse and drain the mushrooms. • Rinse and halve the bell pepper, then remove all stem parts, ribs and seeds. • Cut off the tips of the chicory leaves (about 1½ in.) and arrange in circles on four plates. Shred the rest of the leaves. Slice the mushrooms and cut the bell pepper into strips. • Dribble some of the dressing onto the chicory tips. Combine the rest with the salad, arrange this on the plates and sprinkle the parsley over the salad. • Serve immediately.

Chicory Salad with Raisins

Quick, easy to prepare

Preparation time: 25 minutes

⅓ cup raisins
½ cup hazelnuts
1 lb. chicory
2 egg yolks
2 tbs. cottage cheese
½ tsp. salt
1 pinch each sugar and freshly ground white pepper
1 to 2 tbs. apple vinegar
2 tbs. safflower seed oil
4 leaves fresh peppermint

Soak the raisins in warm water for a few minutes, then rinse and drain. • Coarsely chop the hazelnuts and reserve. • Remove the decayed outer leaves from the chicory, trim the root end, rinse and dry the stalks. Cut out the bitter end of the root since this is where the bitterest parts of chicory are. Shred the chicory and combine with the drained raisins and chopped nuts. • Blend the egg yolks with the cottage cheese, salt, sugar, pepper, vinegar, and oil and toss the dressing with the salad. • Rinse, pat dry and cut the peppermint leaves into strips, then sprinkle over the salad.

Tip: Chicory is also quite tasty with fruit, especially exotic types like cherimoya, dates, kiwis, or mango.

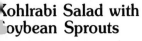

Kohlrabi Salad with Soybean Sprouts

Nutritious, quick

Preparation time: 20 minutes

tbs. sesame seeds	
small bulbs kohlrabi	
red apples	
tbs. lemon juice	
⅓ lb. fresh soybean sprouts	
tbs. apple vinegar	
tbs. maple syrup	
tsp. herbal salt	
tbs. walnut oil	

Roast the sesame seeds in a dry skillet, turning them often, until they give off a pleasant aroma. • Peel the kohlrabi, slice and then cut the slices into sticks. Rinse the tender greens, dry and chop. • Rinse, dry and quarter the apples, then core, slice the quarters and dribble the lemon juice over them. • Blanch the sprouts about 3 minutes in boiling water, drain and combine with the apple, kohlrabi strips and kohlrabi greens. • Blend the vinegar with the syrup, salt and oil. Toss the salad with dressing and sprinkle with the sesame seeds.

Carrot-Kohlrabi Dish

Inexpensive, easy to prepare

Preparation time: 25 minutes
Marinating time: 10 minutes

1 lb. carrots	
3 small kohlrabi bulbs	
2 oz. Gorgonzola cheese	
⅔ cup yogurt	
2 tbs. apple vinegar	
1 pinch each salt and sugar	
1 pinch freshly ground white pepper	
½ handful parsley	
½ cup coarsely chopped walnuts	

Peel, rinse, dry and julienne the carrots. • Peel and slice the kohlrabi, then cut the slices into thin strips. Rinse and chop the tender kohlrabi greens. • Mash the Gorgonzola with a fork and blend with the yogurt. Then add vinegar, salt, sugar and pepper to taste. • Rinse, dry and chop the parsley; combine with the carrot and kohlrabi strips and the dressing. • Marinate covered for 10 minutes and serve sprinkled with the chopped nuts.

Tip: Instead of walnuts, sprinkle 2 tablespoons roasted sunflower seeds over the salad. If the Gorgonzola is a bit too strong in flavor, use cream cheese.

Carrot-Celery Salad

Inexpensive, easy to prepare

Preparation time: 25 minutes

1 egg yolk
1 pinch salt
4 tbs. lemon juice
1 tbs. soy sauce
2 tbs. mango chutney (ready-made)
2 tbs. sunflower seed oil
1 to 2 tsp. honey
Some Tabasco sauce or cayenne pepper
1 lb. carrots
¼ lb. celeriac
1 apple
1 small leek
A few leaves of lettuce

Blend the egg yolk with the salt, lemon juice, soy sauce and chutney. Vigorously blend in the oil. Add honey and tabasco or cayenne to taste for a sweet-and-sour, somewhat hot flavor. • Peel, rinse, and coarsely grate the carrots and celeriac. Combine both with the marinade right away. • Peel the apple and remove the seeds, then grate it, too, and add to the other ingredients. • Use only the white and tender green parts of the leek, cut these into thin rings. Rinse and drain the rings well, then combine with the other prepared ingredients. • Rinse the lettuce leaves, dry and arrange on four plates or a serving platter. Heap the salad on the leaves and serve as soon as possible.

Endive-Clementine Salad

Easy to prepare, quick

Preparation time: 15 minutes

1 head endive
⅔ cup yogurt
1 tsp. mustard
1 tbs. honey
2 tbs. lemon juice
½ cup sunflower seeds
4 clementine oranges

Remove decayed leaves and tough stems from endive and cut into thin strips. Rinse twice (this lettuce is often very sandy) and dry or drain well. •

Blend the yogurt with the mustard, honey and lemon juice. • Combine the endive with the marinade and half of the sunflower seeds and arrange on 4 plates. Sprinkle the remaining sunflower seeds over the salad. • Peel the oranges and either halve, slice or divide into segments. Garnish with the orange pieces.

Tip: Endive salad is also very tasty with this marinade: 3 tablespoons orange juice with 1 tablespoon wine vinegar, ½ teaspoon sweet paprika powder, ½ teaspoon celery salt and 1 teaspoon sugar all blended together, then 4 tablespoons corn oil or sunflower seed oil are vigorously blended in. The marinade should be chilled for 1 hour. Toss with the endive salad right before serving and add 1 sliced banana.

Leek Salad with Bacon

Inexpensive, easy to prepare

Preparation time: 20 minutes

¼ lb. bacon	
3 leeks	
3 tbs. balsamic vinegar	
1 pinch each salt and cayenne pepper	
2 tbs. seed oil	
½ tsp. hot mustard	

Dice the bacon, brown in a pan until crisp and drain on a paper towel. • Cut off the root end and dark green leaf tips from the leeks, halve the stalks, rinse thoroughly and cut into rings. Blanch the leeks 1 minute in a sieve in boiling water, then drain and cool. • Blend the vinegar, salt, cayenne, oil and mustard. Toss the leek with the dressing and add the bacon bits. • Let the leek salad marinate covered until it is served; it tastes best while still warm.

Tip: If desired, add blanched carrot strips and cooked cauliflower florets.

Leek Salad with Apples and Grapes

Inexpensive, easy to prepare

Preparation time: 30 minutes

3 leeks	
12 green and 12 red grapes	
4 apples	
2 tsp. lemon juice	
1 egg yolk	
½ tsp. mustard	
4 tbs. grape seed oil	
2 pinches each salt and freshly ground white pepper	
1 pinch sugar	
1 handful dill	

Remove the root end and dark green leaf tips from the leeks, cut the stalks in half, rinse and cut into rings. Blanch the rings in boiling water, then pour them into a sieve, briefly rinse with cold water and then let them drain. • Rinse, dry, quarter, core and slice the apples. Dribble 1 tablespoon lemon juice over them. • Rinse, halve and remove the seeds from the grapes. • Blend the yolk with the mustard and whisk in the oil, at first drop by drop, then in a thin stream. Add 1 tablespoon lemon juice, salt, pepper, and sugar to taste. • Rinse, dry and chop the dill, add to the dressing. • Combine the drained leek, apple slices and the grape halves (reserve 6 halves of each kind for later). Put a portion on each of 4 plates. Put the dressing over the salad and garnish with the grape halves.

Curly Endive with Radishes

Quick, inexpensive

Preparation time: 20 minutes

1 head curly endive
1 bunch radishes
1 pinch each salt and freshly ground white pepper
4 mandarin oranges
1 small banana
4 tbs. lemon juice
1 tbs. sherry
1 cup sour cream

Cut the curly endive into broad strips, rinse in a sieve and drain. • Trim and rinse the radishes, then slice and combine with the endive, salt and pepper. • Peel the mandarin oranges, skin the segments and cut into pieces. Toss these with the salad. • Peel and mash the banana, then blend it with the lemon juice, sherry, and sour cream. Pour this over the salad.

Tip: This salad is particularly mild in flavor. For a spicier flavor, leave out the mandarin oranges and add thinly sliced onion rings. Then use an oil and vinegar dressing and sprinkle some freshly chopped herbs and green peppercorns over it.

Californian Salad

Quick, easy to prepare

Preparation time: 20 minutes

1 small head iceberg lettuce
4 tomatoes
1 small cucumber
1 red and 1 green bell pepper
¼ lb. canned corn
½ handful dill
⅔ cup crème fraîche
⅔ cup yogurt
2 tbs. sherry vinegar
1 tbs. tomato ketchup
1 pinch each salt and freshly ground white pepper
1 pinch sugar

Remove the decayed outer leaves from the lettuce, tear into smaller pieces, rinse and drain in a sieve. • Rinse and dry the tomatoes, cut into eighths and remove woody parts. • Rinse, dry and thinly slice the cucumber. • Halve the bell peppers and remove all stem parts, ribs and seeds. Rinse the halves, dry and cut into strips. • Drain the corn. • Rinse, dry, and chop the dill, then combine it with the crème fraîche, yogurt, vinegar, ketchup, and spices. • Heap the prepared ingredients in a salad bowl, pour the dill dressing over them, and toss well.

Tip: This side dish can become a whole meal if canned tuna is added.

Yellow Salad

Easy to prepare

Preparation time: 35 minutes

2 medium heads chicory
2 yellow bell peppers
¼ lb. canned corn
2 bunches celery
4 tbs. cottage cheese
1 tsp. honey
1 to 2 tbs. apple vinegar
2 tbs. sunflower seed oil
1 pinch each salt and freshly
ground white pepper
1 pinch sugar
4 tbs. wheat sprouts
2 tbs. linseeds

Remove the outer decayed leaves from the chicory and cut off the root end. Rinse the stalks and cut the bitter wedge out of the root end. • Quarter the bell peppers and remove all stem parts, ribs and seeds. Rinse the halves, dry and cut into strips. • Drain the corn. • Rinse the celery stalks and remove the tough fibers. Then slice the stalks into ¼ inch pieces. • Arrange the vegetables on a platter next to one another or mix in a large bowl. • Blend the cottage cheese with the honey, apple vinegar and sunflower seed oil and add salt, pepper and sugar to taste for a sweet-and-sour flavor. Pour the dressing over the salad. • Rinse the wheat sprouts in a sieve, drain, and sprinkle over the salad with the linseeds.

Mixed Salad

Inexpensive

Preparation time: 30 minutes
Serves: 6 people

1 clove garlic
1 head endive or lollo rosso
1 bunch spring onions
1 lb. tomatoes
2 small zucchini
1 bunch radishes
1 red onion
1 yellow bell pepper
2 stalks celery
3 tbs. herbal vinegar
½ tsp. each salt and pepper
3 tbs. olive oil
1 pinch sugar
1 handful mixed herbs: basil, chives, tarragon

Halve the garlic clove and rub the inside of a large salad bowl with it. • Cut the endive or lollo rosso in broad strips, rinse in a sieve and drain. • Clean, rinse and cut the spring onions into rings. • Rinse and dry the tomatoes, then cut into eighths and remove the stem parts. • Trim, rinse and dry the zucchini and radishes, then slice thinly. • Peel the red onion and cut into thin rings. • Halve the bell pepper, remove all stem parts, ribs and seeds; rinse and cut into strips. • Trim and rinse the celery stalks, then cut into thin slices. • Blend the vinegar with the salt, pepper, oil and sugar. Chop the herbs. • Toss the prepared ingredients with the dressing and sprinkle the herbs over the salad.

Cucumber Salad with Dill

Inexpensive, quick

Preparation time: 20 minutes

2 lbs. cucumber
2 tsp. lemon juice
½ tsp. salt
1 generous pinch each of freshly ground white pepper and sugar
1 tbs. sesame seed oil
½ cup sour cream
1 handful dill

Rub the cucumbers with a dry cloth, then rinse and dry. Slice the cucumber and cut into strips. • Blend the lemon juice with the salt, pepper and sugar, add the sesame seed oil and the sour cream and toss this dressing with the salad. • Rinse, dry, and chop the dill. Serve the salad sprinkled with the dill.

Tip: Several herbs go well with cucumber salad, like borage, pimpernel, rosemary, or peppermint. Instead of sour cream, use sweet cream or crème fraîche, or even just a vinegar and oil dressing. For an especially spicy flavor, add thinly sliced pepperoni and some paprika powder to the salad.

Tunisian Paprika Salad

Easy to prepare

Preparation time: 40 minutes
Marinating time: 30 minutes

1½ lbs. green bell peppers
2 pepperoni peppers
2 onions
3 cloves garlic
6 tbs. olive oil
1 lb. ripe, firm tomatoes
1 tsp. salt
2 to 3 pinches freshly ground black pepper
2 tsp. finely chopped basil

Rinse and dry the bell peppers and pepperoni peppers, then place them on a baking sheet under the broiler, turning frequently, until the skin darkens and bursts. • Peel and chop the onions and garlic, then add both to the olive oil. • Peel the bell peppers and the pepperoni peppers, halve them, remove all stem parts, seeds and ribs and dice the halves. • Slit the bottom ends of the tomatoes crosswise and par-boil briefly. As soon as the tomato skin comes off easily, rinse them in cold water, peel and dice. Add any juice or seeds to the dressing. • Combine the bell pepper pieces and tomato with the oil-onion-garlic mixture. • Marinate the salad, covered, in the refrigerator for 30 minutes and serve sprinkled with the pepper and basil.

Dandelion Salad with Green Rye

Nutritious, easy to prepare

Soaking time: 12 hours
Preparation time: 30 minutes
Marinating time: 10 minutes

lb. green rye	
small bay leaf	
tsp. granulated chicken bouillon	
tbs. soy sauce	
tbs. red wine vinegar	
tbs. olive oil	
to 2 pinches freshly ground black pepper	
-½ lb. dandelion greens	
red onion	
cup yogurt	
cup sour cream	
tsp. mustard	
black olives	
tsp. sea salt, if needed	

Soak the green rye in a pint of water overnight. • Boil the rye in the soaking water for about 15 minutes with the bay leaf and the chicken bouillon, drain in a sieve and remove the bay leaf. • Combine the rye kernels with the soy sauce, vinegar, pepper, and oil in a bowl. • Pick out the decayed leaves and tough stems from the dandelion, rinse well, drain and cut into fine strips. • Peel and quarter the onion, then slice thinly. • Blend the sour cream, yogurt, and mustard and combine with the chopped ingredients and the kernels. Pit the olives, coarsely chop, combine with the salad and then let the salad marinate for about 10 minutes.

Dandelion Salad with Azuki Beans

Nutritious, easy to prepare

Soaking time: 12 hours
Preparation time: 40 minutes
Marinating time: 10 minutes

⅓ lb. azuki beans	
1 bay leaf	
2 tsp. granulated vegetable broth	
¼-½ lb. dandelion greens	
2 shallots	
1 red onion	
2 or 3 yellow or red tomatoes	
5 to 6 tbs. red wine vinegar	
5 to 6 tbs. olive oil	
1 tsp. salt	
1-2 pinches freshly ground black pepper	

Soak the azuki beans overnight in 3 cups water. • Boil them in the soaking water with the bay leaf and the broth for about 30 minutes, then drain and allow to cool in a sieve; remove the bay leaf. • Pick out the decayed leaves and tough stems from the dandelion, remove root end, rinse thoroughly, drain and cut into fine strips. Peel the shallots and onion. Chop the shallots; quarter the onion and thinly slice the quarters. • Rinse and cut the tomatoes into eighths, and remove any woody stem parts. • Combine the prepared ingredients in a bowl. Blend a dressing of the vinegar, oil, salt and pepper, and pour this over the beans, dandelion, and shallots. Marinate for 10 minutes.

Wax Bean Salad with Egg

Easy to prepare

Preparation time: 30 minutes
Marinating time: 15 minutes

1 lb. yellow wax beans
¼ tsp. salt
1 hard-boiled egg
1 onion
2 tbs. white wine vinegar
¼ to ½ tsp. mild mustard
1 pinch each salt and freshly ground white pepper
4 tbs. sunflower seed oil
2 tbs. freshly chopped parsley

Rinse the beans in lukewarm water, drain, and pull off fibers, if necessary. Halve or quarter larger beans. Cover the beans in salted water and simmer, covered, for 15 minutes over low heat. • Peel and chop the egg. Peel and chop the onion. • Drain the cooked beans in a sieve and let cool. • Whisk together the vinegar, mustard, salt, pepper and oil. • Combine the drained beans with the onion and the dressing in a bowl and marinate, covered, for 15 minutes. • Sprinkle the egg and parsley over the salad right before serving.

Tip: Fine bean salads can also be made using young green string beans. Try it with a vinaigrette sauce and add some garlic, if desired.

Mediterranean Radicchio Salad

Inexpensive, easy to prepare

Preparation time: 25 minutes

¾ lb. radicchio lettuce
¼ lb. chervil
3 fresh purslane leaves
2 cloves garlic
1 piece of bread crust
2 hard-boiled eggs
2 tbs. vinegar (fruit-based)
1 tsp. mustard
¼ tsp. salt
1 pinch freshly ground black pepper
4 tbs. olive oil

Separate the leaves of the radicchio and wash in water several times, then dry. Discard decayed parts and tear the large leaves. • Rinse and dry the chervil and purslane leaves as well. Chop the purslane a little smaller than the chervil, remove the tough stems from the chervil. Combine the herbs with the lettuce. • Peel the garlic cloves. Halve one clove and rub it into the bread crust. Then cut the crust into very small pieces and toss with the salad. Crush the rest of the garlic into a small bowl. • Peel and chop the eggs • Blend the vinegar with the mustard, salt, pepper and oil. Toss the salad with the dressing and sprinkle the egg over it.

Field Salad with Radicchio

Inexpensive, easy to prepare

Preparation time: 25 minutes

¼ lb. wild greens	
1 head radicchio	
3 mandarin oranges	
1 small white onion	
1 small apple	
3 tbs. apple vinegar	
½ to 1 tsp. herb salt	
1 tsp. maple syrup	
1 pinch freshly ground white pepper	
2 tbs. walnut oil	

Discard decayed leaves and tough stems from the wild greens, rinse well and drain. • Separate the leaves of the radicchio, tear the leaves into pieces, rinse (in a sieve) and drain. • Peel the mandarin oranges, remove the seeds and peel the segments, then halve each segment. • Peel and chop the onion. • Combine all prepared ingredients in a bowl. • Quarter the apple, core and grate, then blend the grated apple with the apple vinegar, herb salt, syrup, pepper, and oil. Toss the salad with the dressing.

Tip: Instead of mandarin oranges, you could use thinly sliced mushrooms. The dressing would then be made of lemon juice, wheat seed oil, salt and pepper.

Radicchio with Roquefort Dressing

Quick, easy to prepare

Preparation time: 20 minutes
Marinating time: 10 minutes

1 large head radicchio	
1 handful garden cress	
¼ lb. walnuts	
¼ lb. Roquefort cheese	
1 tbs. red wine vinegar	
⅓ lb. yogurt	
1 pinch salt	
1 pinch freshly ground black pepper	

Separate the leaves of the radicchio, tear them into pieces, rinse in a sieve and drain. • Rinse the garden cress, pat dry and chop. • Coarsely chop the walnuts. • Mash the Roquefort with a fork and blend with the vinegar, yogurt, salt and pepper. • Combine the radicchio with the cress and the nuts in a bowl, toss with the dressing and marinate, covered, for 10 minutes.

Tip: To emphasize the flavor of the radicchio, grate the peeled root and combine it with the salad. Instead of Roquefort, use any other similar cheese, like Gorgonzola or Bavarian blue.

Chinese Cabbage with Grapes

Nutritious, inexpensive

Preparation time: 30 minutes

⅓ cup sesame seeds
¼ lb. green grapes
¼ lb. dark red grapes
½ lb. Chinese cabbage
¼ lb. wild greens
2 tbs. lemon juice
2 tsp. honey
1 pinch freshly ground ginger
1 pinch freshly ground white pepper
1 pinch ground cloves
2 tbs. sesame seed oil

Roast the sesame seeds in a dry pan, while turning frequently; continue until they darken slightly and begin to give off a pleasant aroma. Set the roasted seeds aside. • Pick the grapes from the stems, rinse, halve, and remove seeds. • Discard root ends and decayed leaves from the Chinese cabbage, rinse, drain well, and cut into strips. • Rinse, pick over and drain the wild greens. • Blend the lemon juice with the honey, ginger, pepper and ground cloves. Add the sesame seed oil. Toss all the prepared ingredients, except for the sesame seeds, with the dressing, then sprinkle the seeds over the salad.

Tip: Replace the sesame seeds and oil with either walnuts and walnut oil or sunflower seeds and their oil.

Green Asparagus Salad

Easy to prepare, needs some time

Preparation time: 45 minutes
Marinating time: 30 minutes

2 lbs. green asparagus
1 tsp. salt
1 lump sugar
½ lb. small mushrooms
1 tbs. butter
2 pinches salt
2 or 3 firm tomatoes
3 tbs. wine vinegar
1 pinch each freshly ground white pepper and hot paprika powder
5 tbs. olive oil
2 tbs. freshly chopped parsley

Rinse the asparagus and cut off the woody ends. Bundle the asparagus stalks 6 at a time. Bring enough water (with the salt and lump of sugar) to boil to cover the asparagus. Cook the asparagus covered for 15 to 20 minutes. • Clean, rinse and thinly slice the mushrooms, then sauté for 10 minutes in the butter. Let cool and salt lightly. • Parboil the tomatoes, peel, halve and remove all stem parts and seeds. Dice the halves. • Drain the asparagus, cut into 2-inch pieces and combine with the mushrooms and tomato in a bowl. • Blend a dressing from the vinegar, the remaining salt, pepper, paprika powder, and oil, then pour this over the vegetables. Toss the salad and sprinkle with the parsley. • Marinate for 30 minutes.

Piquant Zucchini Salad

Inexpensive, easy to prepare

Preparation time: 25 minutes

1 lb. zucchini	
1½ qts. water	
½ tsp. salt	
ice cubes	
1 onion	
4 small ripe tomatoes	
4 tbs. diced canned pumpkin	
2 tbs. herbal vinegar	
1 tbs. pumpkin juice	
1 pinch each salt, sugar, and freshly ground white pepper	
1 small clove garlic	
4 tbs. olive oil	
2 tbs. chopped chives	

Rub the zucchini with a kitchen towel, rinse in lukewarm water and dry. Slice the unpeeled zucchini in medium slices, removing stem and root ends while you are doing this. • Bring the salted water to a boil and blanch the zucchini (in a sieve) for about 2 minutes. Immerse the zucchini in iced water and drain. • Peel and dice the onion • Rinse and dry the tomatoes, cut them into eighths, remove any stem parts. • Drain and chop the pumpkin cubes. • Blend the vinegar, pumpkin juice, pepper, sugar and salt. Peel the garlic and crush into a bowl. Blend this with the vinegar mixture and whisk in the oil. • Toss the dressing with the salad, arrange the salad for serving and sprinkle the chives over it.

Salad with Artichoke Hearts

Easy to prepare

Preparation time: 25 minutes

½ lb. Boston lettuce	
½ lb. radicchio	
¼ lb. wild greens	
2 small onions	
½ lb. canned artichoke hearts	
1 large clove garlic	
2 tbs. white wine vinegar	
1 pinch each salt, sugar, and white pepper	
4 tbs. sunflower seed oil	
2 tbs. mixed herbs, freshly chopped	

Separate the leaves of the radicchio and the Boston lettuce and rinse several times. Rinse the wild greens several times. Dry the leaves. • Peel the onions and cut into thin rings. • Drain and quarter the artichoke hearts. • Peel the garlic clove and crush into a small bowl. • Blend the salt, pepper and sugar into the vinegar, until all grains have dissolved. Combine the vinegar mixture with the garlic and whisk in the oil. • Arrange the leafy salads in a bowl, add the artichoke hearts and onion rings over them, and dribble the dressing over the salad. • Sprinkle the chopped herbs over the salad and serve as soon as possible.

Red Cabbage Salad with Pumpkin Seeds

Easy to prepare, needs some time

Preparation time: 20 minutes
Marinating time: 1 hour

1 small head red cabbage
1 qt. water
½ tsp. salt
2 tbs. vinegar
4 tbs. lemon juice
2 tbs. honey
1 pinch freshly ground black pepper
4 tbs. walnut oil
⅓ to ½ cup pumpkin seeds
¼ lb. feta cheese

Discard the outer leaves of cabbage. Quarter the cabbage and cut away the stem. Shred the cabbage. • Bring the water with salt and vinegar to a boil, blanch the cabbage for 1 minute and drain well in a sieve. • Blend the lemon juice, honey, pepper and oil. Toss the cabbage with the marinade and marinate covered for 1 hour. • Roast the pumpkin seeds in a dry pan for 1 minute, turning frequently. • Crumble the feta and sprinkle it with the pumpkin seeds over the salad.

Tip: Red cabbage salad is also quite tasty with a cranberry dressing. Combine 2 tablespoons vinegar with 1 teaspoon lemon juice, 2 tablespoons cranberry preserves and 6 tablespoons oil. Add 1 sliced apple and toss with the salad.

Field Salad with Bacon

Easy to prepare, inexpensive

Preparation time: 20 minutes

4 slices bacon (about 2 oz.)
1 medium onion
2 tbs. oil
½ lb. wild greens
1 bunch chicory
1 pinch salt
1 pinch freshly ground black pepper
4 tbs. lemon juice
1 handful chives

Cut the bacon into thin strips. Peel and dice the onion. • Heat the oil in a pan. Sauté the bacon and onion over medium heat until the bacon is crispy. Put the bacon-onion mixture in a salad bowl to cool. • Discard any decayed leaves or tough stems from the wild greens, rinse and dry. • Cut off the root end of the chicory and make a wedge-shaped cut into the stalk to remove the bitter end. Rinse, drain, and cut the chicory into rings. Add the chicory and greens to the salad bowl. • Salt and pepper to taste and dribble the lemon juice over the salad. Toss gently with the bacon and onions. • Rinse the chives, chop and sprinkle over the salad. Serve the salad soon after it is made.

Chinese Cabbage with Feta Cheese

Inexpensive, quick

Preparation time: 30 minutes
Marinating time: 1 hour

1 large onion (about ½ lb.)
4 tbs. olive oil
2 sprigs fresh or ½ tsp. dried thyme
4 to 6 tbs. wine vinegar
2 pinches each salt and freshly ground black pepper
1⅔ lb. firm Chinese cabbage
½ lb. feta cheese

Peel, halve and dice the onion. • Heat the olive oil and sauté the onion in it briefly, until it is translucent. Put the onion with the oil into a salad bowl. • Rinse and dry the thyme, pick off the leaves and chop them. Add the thyme (dry or fresh) to the onion while it is still warm. Add the wine vinegar and salt and pepper to taste. • Remove the outer leaves from the cabbage, rinse the cabbage, drain, and halve lengthwise. Remove the stem and shred. Combine the shredded cabbage with the prepared ingredients and toss gently. • Cube or crumble the feta and add to the salad. • Marinate covered for at least 1 hour. • The salad can be made ahead of time and will stay fresh in the refrigerator for 1 or 2 days.

Russian Red Beet Salad

Easy to prepare, inexpensive

Preparation time: 1¾ hours
Final touches: 30 minutes

3 medium red beets
2 large tart apples
2 tbs. lemon juice
1 cup heavy cream
2 tbs. freshly grated horseradish
½ tsp. salt
½ tsp. freshly ground black pepper
½ tsp. freshly ground caraway seeds

Brush the beets under running water, cover with water and bring to a boil. Simmer for 1½ hours over medium heat, pour into a sieve when done, rinse with cold water and peel. Slice the beets, then dice. • Peel, quarter and core the apples. Dice the apple quarters and dribble some lemon juice over them to avoid discoloration. • Whip the cream until semi-stiff and combine with the grated horseradish. Add salt, pepper, and ground caraway to the horseradish-cream mixture to taste. • Combine the apples, beets and dressing in a bowl.

Broccoli Salad with Radishes

Easy to prepare

Preparation time: 45 minutes
Marinating time: 10 minutes

1¾ lbs. broccoli
1 tsp. salt
2 eggs
1 small leek
1 firm tomato
5 to 6 radishes
1 pickled green pepper
3 tbs. wine vinegar
1 pinch each salt, black pepper and grated nutmeg
½ tsp. sugar
1 tsp. hot mustard
6 tbs. olive oil
2 tbs. chopped chives
2 tbs. freshly chopped parsley

Rinse the broccoli and separate into florets. Cut off the stems, peel and cut into equal-sized pieces. Cover these with lightly salted water and simmer for 6 minutes. Then add the florets and cook for another 6 minutes. Transfer the broccoli to a sieve, drain and cool. • Pierce the eggs at the large end with a needle, lay them into boiling water and cook for 8 minutes. Rinse briefly under cold water, peel and cool. • Remove the dark green tips of the leaves and the root ends from the leek. Halve lengthwise, rinse and slice into rings. • Rinse and halve the tomato; remove the woody parts and seeds and slice. Dice the flesh. • Rinse and trim the radishes, then chop coarsely. • Dice the green pepper. • Blend a dressing from the wine vinegar, salt, pepper, nutmeg, sugar, mustard, and olive oil. Toss the prepared ingredients with the dressing and chopped herbs. Marinate for 10 minutes. • Chop the eggs and sprinkle them over the salad.

Tyrolean Cabbage Salad

Inexpensive, easy to prepare

Preparation time: 30 minutes

1½ lbs. white cabbage

1 tsp. salt

1 pinch freshly ground white pepper

1 tsp. caraway seeds

⅓ lb. bacon

2 tbs. oil

3 to 4 tbs. wine vinegar

Discard any decayed cabbage leaves. Quarter the head of cabbage and remove the stem. Rinse the quarters, drain and shred, then place in a bowl. Sprinkle salt over the cabbage and knead well, until the cabbage is tender and juicy. Add pepper and caraway to taste. • Cut the bacon into small pieces. Heat the oil in a skillet and fry the bacon until it is crisp. Remove the skillet from heat and pour in the vinegar. Pour the hot oil-vinegar-bacon sauce over the salad and toss well.

Tip: In Tyrol, this salad is often served with pork roast and dumplings.

Savoy Cabbage Salad

Inexpensive, easy to prepare

Preparation time: 45 minutes
Marinating time: 30 minutes

2 lbs. savoy cabbage

1 qt. water

1 tsp. salt

Juice of 1 lemon

1 pinch each salt and freshly ground pepper

1 pinch freshly grated nutmeg

6 tbs. olive oil

Discard the tough outer leaves of the cabbage. Quarter the head and rinse in cold water. Place the cabbage in the quart of salted water, bring to a boil and cook for 30 minutes until just done. Drain the quarters well and cut into 1 inch wide strips while still hot. • Blend the lemon juice, salt, nutmeg, and pepper in a salad bowl, then whisk in the oil. Toss the warm cabbage with the dressing. Marinate for at least 30 minutes and let cool.

Tip: The savoy cabbage salad can be made attractive for eye and palate by adding 2 chopped, hard-boiled eggs. A little garlic can also be added.

Mushroom Salad with Watercress

Easy to prepare

Preparation time: 20 minutes

1 bunch watercress
1 lb. small mushrooms
2 shallots
1 clove garlic
4 tbs. balsamic vinegar
2 pinches each salt and freshly ground black pepper
1 tsp. dried tarragon
⅛ tsp. mustard
6 tbs. olive oil

Discard any decayed or large tough leaves of the watercress. Pick out the tender leaves, rinse and dry. • Clean, rinse and quarter the mushrooms. • Peel and chop the shallots and garlic. • Blend the vinegar, salt, pepper, tarragon, mustard, shallots and garlic. Add the olive oil and whisk well until blended. • Pour the dressing over the mushrooms and cress, toss well, and serve immediately with a baguette or rolls.

Green Bean Salad with Horseradish

Inexpensive, easy to prepare

Preparation time: 15 minutes
Marinating time: 3½ hours
Final preparation: 10 minutes

1 lb. tender green beans
1 tsp. salt
3 sprigs summer savory
1 onion
4 tbs. herbal vinegar
4 tbs. sunflower seed oil
1 pinch each salt and pepper
3 tbs. mayonnaise
3 tbs. sour cream
1 tsp. freshly grated horseradish
1 tsp. lemon juice
½ tsp. mustard powder

Clean the beans, removing any strings, if necessary. Just barely cover in water, add salt and savory. Bring to a boil and simmer. Cook for about 10 to 15 minutes. Pour into a sieve, rinse quickly with cold water and drain. • Peel the onion and slice into rings. • Blend the vinegar and oil. Add salt, pepper, and onion rings. Put the beans into the bowl with the dressing and marinate for 3 hours. • Blend the mayonnaise, sour cream, horseradish, lemon juice and mustard powder. Pour this dressing over the beans and marinate another 30 minutes.
Tip: Instead of fresh horseradish, substitute double the amount of canned horseradish.

Brussels Sprout Salad with Apple

Inexpensive, easy to prepare

Preparation time: 35 minutes

1¼ lbs. small Brussels sprouts
2 cups water
1 tsp. salt
1 large apple
2 tsp. lemon juice
½ ripe banana
1 pinch each salt and freshly ground white pepper
4 tbs. crème fraîche
Milk
3 fresh sage leaves

Discard any decayed leaves from the Brussels sprouts and trim the stems. Rinse the sprouts in lukewarm water and drain. Bring the salted water to a boil. Steam the Brussels sprouts covered for 20 minutes. • In the meantime, peel, core, and dice the apple. Dribble the lemon juice over the apple pieces. • Peel the banana, mash it with a fork and combine with the salt, pepper, and crème fraîche; if needed, add some milk to make the dressing more liquid. • Rinse, dry, and cut the sage leaves into strips. • Let the Brussels sprouts drain and cool. Halve or quarter the larger florets. • Combine the sprouts with the apple and toss with the dressing. Scatter the sage over the salad before serving.

Cauliflower and Broccoli Salad

Easy to prepare, quick

Preparation time: 30 minutes

1½ tsp. salt
1 cauliflower (about 1 lb.)
1 lb. broccoli
1 slice of white bread
4 tbs. milk
⅓ cup blanched almonds
1 clove garlic
6 tbs. lemon juice
1 pinch grated nutmeg
1 pinch freshly ground white pepper
2 tbs. olive oil
1 handful parsley

Bring 2 quarts water (with 1 teaspoon salt) to a boil. • Trim the cauliflower, separate into florets and rinse. • Trim the broccoli in a similar manner, cutting the florets from the stems. Peel the stems and slice them. Rinse the broccoli. • Cook the cauliflower 5 minutes in the boiling water, add the broccoli and cook another 2 minutes. Briefly rinse the vegetables under cold water and drain. • Soak the white bread in the milk (do this on a plate). • Puree the almonds, the soaked bread, and the peeled garlic clove in a blender. In a bowl, blend the puree with the lemon juice, 3 tablespoons water, ½ teaspoon salt, the nutmeg, pepper and oil until dressing is thick. • Rinse, dry and finely chop the parsley, then stir it into the dressing. • Arrange the florets on four plates and give a quarter of the dressing to each serving.

Coleslaw

American specialty, easy to prepare

Preparation time: 30 minutes
Marinating time: 1 hour

1 white cabbage (about 1¼ lb.)
10 oz. carrots
⅓ cup raisins
1 egg yolk
½ tsp. mustard
4 tbs. sunflower seed oil
1 tbs. white wine vinegar
2 pinches each sugar, salt and freshly ground black pepper

Discard the outer cabbage leaves, quarter the cabbage and cut out the stem. Shred the cabbage. • Trim and peel the carrots. Wash and grate coarsely. • Rinse the raisins under hot water and drain. • Blend the yolk with the mustard and oil, add the latter drop by drop, then in a thin stream, until it is a thick sauce. Blend in the vinegar and then add salt, pepper and sugar to taste. If necessary, add some milk or water to make the dressing more liquid. • Combine the shredded cabbage, grated carrots, drained raisins and the dressing in a bowl and toss well. • Marinate covered for at least 1 hour.

Tip: Coleslaw most often accompanies sautéed dishes, or it serves as a picnic salad. Of course, it also appears at any self-respecting barbecue.

Potato Salad with Cucumber

Inexpensive, easy to prepare

Preparation time: 40 minutes
Marinating time: 20 minutes

| 1¾ lbs. potatoes (should stay firm after cooking) |
| 2 cups water |
| 1 tsp. salt |
| 1¼ lbs. cucumbers |
| 1 large onion |
| 1 to 2 tbs. lemon juice |
| 2 pinches each salt and freshly ground white pepper |
| 2 pinches sugar |
| 1 to 2 tsp. maple syrup |
| 3 tbs. chopped chives |

Brush the potatoes well under running water. Then bring the potatoes and salted water to a boil. Cook the potatoes covered for about 25 minutes. • Rub the cucumbers with a kitchen towel, rinse in lukewarm water, dry and use a grater to slice. • Peel and chop the onion. • The potatoes are done when a fork goes in easily. Pour off the water, let the potatoes steam themselves dry a little, then peel and slice them while they are still hot. • Combine the sliced potatoes with the onion, sliced cucumbers, lemon juice, salt, pepper and sugar. Add additional seasoning to taste. Add enough maple syrup to give the salad a pleasantly sweet-and-sour flavor. • Marinate covered for 20 minutes at room temperature and sprinkle the chives over the salad before serving.

Simple Potato Salad

Inexpensive, easy to prepare

Preparation time: 40 minutes
Marinating time: 25 minutes

| 1¾ lbs. potatoes (should stay firm after cooking) |
| 2 cups water |
| 1 tsp. salt |
| 2 onions |
| 1½ cups cold beef broth |
| 2 tbs. white wine vinegar |
| ½ tsp. salt |
| 2 pinches freshly ground white pepper |
| 5 tbs. sunflower seed oil |
| 2 tbs. freshly chopped parsley |

Brush the potatoes well under running water and bring to a boil in the salted water. Simmer covered over low heat for about 25 minutes. • Peel and chop the onions. • The potatoes are done when a fork goes in easily. Pour out the water when the potatoes are done and let them steam themselves dry briefly, then peel and slice them while they are still hot. • Toss the beef broth and vinegar with the warm potatoes. Salt and pepper to taste. Toss the salad with the oil and marinate covered at room temperature for about 25 minutes. • Sprinkle the chopped parsley over the salad before serving.

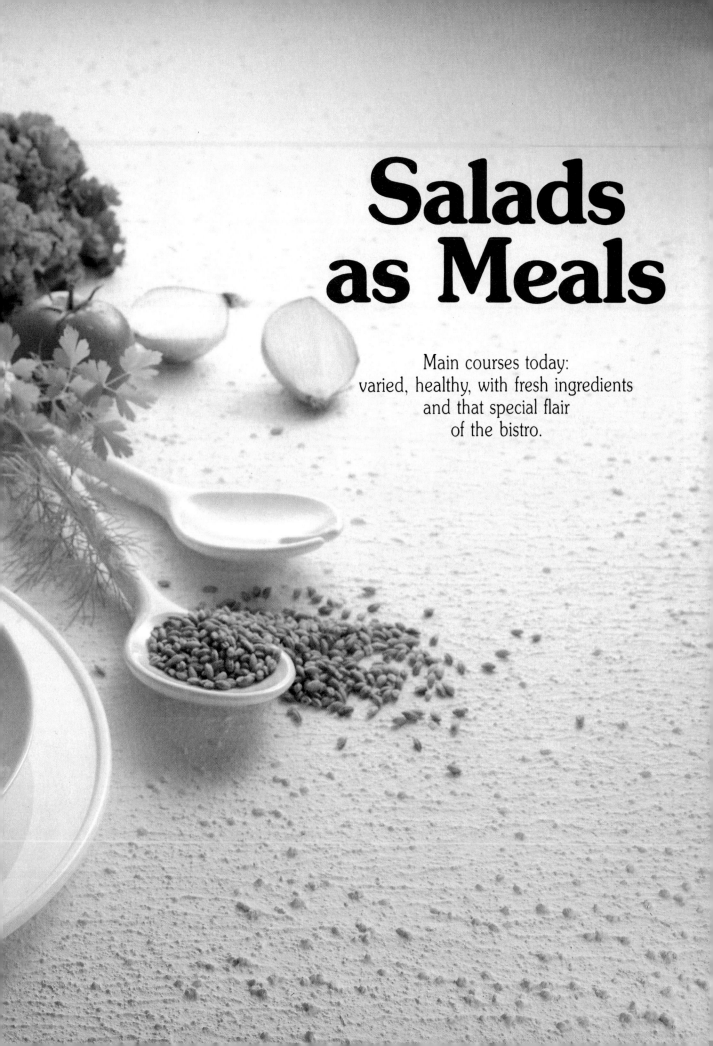

Salads as Meals

Main courses today:
varied, healthy, with fresh ingredients
and that special flair
of the bistro.

Pompadour Salad

Takes some time

Preparation time: 1 hour
Marinating time: 30 minutes

1¾ lbs. potatoes (should stay firm when cooked)

1 lb. celeriac (knob celery)

1 pint water

1 tsp. salt

1 lb. cauliflower florets

5 tbs. mayonnaise

5 tbs. cream

1 tbs. mild mustard

1 pinch each salt and freshly ground white pepper

1 pinch ground mace

Rinse the potatoes and celeriac well. Boil the potatoes (with ½ teaspoon salt) in the water, covered, for about 25 minutes. • Peel the celeriac, rinse again and dice. Cook the celeriac pieces in a covered pot with ½ teaspoon salt, in enough water to cover, for about 25 minutes. • Rinse the cauliflower florets and cook them in a covered pot, in enough water to cover, over low heat for 15 minutes. • Pour out the potatoes, peel and cube. • Drain the celeriac and cauliflower in a sieve and allow to cool. • Blend the mayonnaise with the cream, mustard, salt, pepper, and mace. • Combine the potatoes, cauliflower, celeriac and dressing in a bowl and marinate for 30 minutes.

Italian Salad

Needs some time

Preparation time: 1 hour

1¼ lbs. potatoes (should stay firm after cooking)

1½ tsp. salt

½ lb. green beans

½ lb. peas

½ lb. young carrots

1 lb. small ripe tomatoes

12 black olives

4 anchovy fillets

4 tbs. mayonnaise

4 tbs. yogurt

2 pinches each of salt, freshly ground black pepper, and hot paprika powder

2 tbs. small capers

Rinse the potatoes and boil them in ½ quart water, covered, salted with ½ teaspoon salt for about 25 minutes. • Trim and rinse the beans. Halve the larger beans. Cook the beans in a little salted water, covered, for 15 minutes. • Rinse the peas. Peel, rinse, and dice the carrots. Cook the peas and carrots in enough water to cover (and ½ teaspoon salt) for 10 minutes. • Pour out the potatoes, peel and cube them. Drain the beans. • Pour the peas and carrots into a sieve. • Peel the tomatoes, dice, removing any stem parts, reserve seeds and juices. • Combine the vegetables with the olives. • Chop the anchovy. • Blend the mayonnaise with the yogurt, spices, anchovies and tomato juice. Toss the dressing with the salad and sprinkle the capers over the salad.

Potato Salad with Fennel

Inexpensive, easy to prepare

Preparation time: 40 minutes

2 lbs. potatoes (should stay firm after cooking)
1 fennel bulb
1 sour apple
⅓ lb. smoked pork, lightly salted
4 tbs. mayonnaise
½ lb. sour cream
1 pinch each salt and freshly ground black pepper
1 tbs. red wine vinegar
1 handful mixed herbs: chervil, chives, and sage
1 small onion

Brush the potatoes well under running water, bring to a boil in enough water to cover and cook 25 to 30 minutes. • Remove the outer, harder ribs from the fennel bulb, rinse and quarter the fennel, then slice thinly. Reserve some of the fennel greens. • Peel, quarter, core and dice the apple. • Slice the ham in thin strips. • Blend the mayonnaise, sour cream, salt, pepper, and vinegar. Rinse, pat dry, pick over, and chop the herbs. Peel and grate the onion, then blend it and the herbs into the dressing. • Drain the potatoes, let cool, peel and slice. Combine the sliced potato with the fennel, apple, and ham. Toss the salad with the dressing.

Tip: Instead of the ham, also try 2 diced pickled white herring.

Potato Salad with Radishes

Easy to prepare, inexpensive

Preparation time: 40 minutes
Marinating time: 1 hour

2 lbs. potatoes (should stay firm after cooking)
1 pint water
½ tsp. salt
1 cucumber
2 bunches radishes
1 onion
4 tbs. herbal vinegar
2 pinches each salt and freshly ground white pepper
1 tsp. mustard
1 pinch sugar
6 tbs. sunflower seed oil
4 hard-boiled eggs

Brush the potatoes well under running water, then cook them in salted water for 20 to 25 minutes. • Rinse, dry, peel and dice the cucumber. • Rinse, dry and trim the radishes, then quarter. • Peel and chop the onion, then blend it with the vinegar, salt, pepper, mustard, sugar and oil. • Drain the potatoes, let cool slightly, then peel and slice. • Combine the potatoes, cucumber and radishes with the dressing, then toss and marinate for 1 hour. • Arrange the salad on a platter. Peel the eggs and cut them into eighths and scatter over the salad.

Potato Salad with Red Beets

Nutritious, inexpensive

Preparation time: 1 hour and 10 minutes
Marinating time: 10 minutes

½ lb. red beets
¾ lb. potatoes (should stay firm after cooking)
½ lb. sour apples
⅓ lb. pickles
1 onion
2 tsp. granulated vegetable bouillon
2 tbs. apple vinegar
2 tsp. mustard
1 pinch freshly ground black pepper
2 tbs. safflower seed oil
1 box garden cress

Rinse the red beets, cut off the leaf stems 1 inch from the beet, if necessary, then cook in enough water to cover for about 15 minutes. • Brush the potatoes well under running water and add them to the cooking beets. Cook the beets and potatoes together for 20 to 30 minutes. Pour off the water, rinse the vegetables in cold water and allow to cool somewhat. • Peel the beets and potatoes, then finely dice the beets, the potatoes a little less so. • Rinse, quarter, core, and dice the apples. • Dice the pickles. Peel and chop the onion. • Bring ½ cup water to a boil, dissolve the vegetable bouillon in it and then combine the bouillon with the prepared ingredients in a bowl. • Blend the vinegar, mustard, pepper and oil and toss with the salad. Marinate for about 10 minutes. • Cut off the cress, rinse, dry and toss with the salad.

Potato Salad with Buckwheat

Nutritious, takes some time

Preparation time: 50 minutes
Marinating time: 10 minutes

¾ lb. potatoes
2 tsp. oil
2 tsp. granulated vegetable bouillon
2 tsp. dried marjoram
1 bay leaf
2 oz. buckwheat
2 oz. red lentils
⅓ lb. peas
3 shallots
½ cup sour cream
2 tbs. each estragon vinegar and olive oil
1 tsp. salt
1 pinch freshly ground black pepper
2 tomatoes
2 tbs. chopped chives

Brush the potatoes well under running water, cook until done in a little water, rinse briefly in cold water, then peel and dice. • In the meantime, bring 3 cups water with 2 teaspoons oil, 2 teaspoons granulated vegetable bouillon, 1 teaspoon marjoram, and the bay leaf to a boil. Sprinkle in the buckwheat and lentils and cook for 10 minutes. Then add the peas and cook another 10 minutes. Drain in a sieve and remove the bay leaf. • Peel and slice the shallots into thin rings. • Blend the sour cream, oil, vinegar, salt, pepper, and remaining marjoram and blend this dressing with the prepared ingredients. • Rinse the tomatoes, cut into eighths and, with the chives, toss with the salad. Marinate for 10 minutes.

Green Kale Salad with Soybeans

Nutritious, takes some time

Soaking time: 12 hours
Preparation time: 2 hours
Marinating time: 10 minutes

¼ lb. yellow soybeans

1 tsp. granulated vegetable bouillon

1 bay leaf

1 lb. green kale

⅓ lb. fresh soybean sprouts

1 red onion

3 tbs. each safflower seed oil and red wine vinegar

2 tbs. soy sauce

1 or 2 pinches freshly ground black pepper

Soak the soybeans overnight in 1 pint water. • Cook the beans in 1 pint fresh water with the vegetable bouillon and the bay leaf for just barely 2 hours, then drain in a sieve and remove the bay leaf. • While waiting for the beans to cook, rinse the kale well, discard the stems and tough parts and blanch the leaves for 10 minutes in boiling water. Drain the leaves in a sieve, allowing them to cool somewhat, then coarsely chop them. • Rinse the sprouts well, blanch for 5 minutes in boiling water and drain. • Peel and halve the onion lengthwise, then thinly slice. • Combine the drained, warm beans with the kale and the oil, vinegar, soy sauce and onion in a bowl, tossing well. Pepper to taste. • Marinate for about 10 minutes. • This salad tastes best while still warm.

Vegetable Noodle Salad

Inexpensive, easy to prepare

Preparation time: 40 minutes
Marinating time: 30 minutes
Serves: 6 people

½ lb. elbow macaroni
1 tsp. salt
2½ qts. water
½ lb. carrots
½ lb. green beans
3 pinches salt
3 tomatoes
⅔ lb. frozen peas
2 small zucchini
3 tbs. mayonnaise
1 cup sour cream
3 tbs. (fruit-based) vinegar
1 tsp. salt
½ tsp. black pepper
1 pinch sugar
1 handful parsley
1 handful chives

Cook the noodles "al dente" in boiling salted water for 8 to 10 minutes, then pour them into a sieve, rinse briefly and drain. • Rinse, peel and dice the carrots. Trim and rinse the beans, then cut them into small pieces. Cook the beans and carrots in a little water with 2 pinches salt for 15 minutes. • Rinse and dry the tomatoes, then cut them into eighths, removing the stem parts. • Cook the peas in 1 cup water with 1 pinch salt for 5 minutes. • Trim, rinse, dry and slice the zucchini. • Blend the mayonnaise, sour cream, vinegar, salt, pepper, and sugar. Rinse and dry the parsley and chives. Chop the parsley and add it to the dressing. • Drain the cooked vegetables and allow to cool somewhat, then combine them with the noodles, tomatoes and zucchini. Toss with the dressing. • Chop the chives and sprinkle over the salad. Marinate covered for 30 minutes.

ettuce and Tuna

**asy to
repare, inexpensive**

reparation time: 20 minutes

eggs
onion (about 1 lb.)
pinches salt
heads Boston lettuce
lb. canned, drained tuna
/2 tbs. wine vinegar
tsp. mustard
pinch freshly ground white
epper
tbs. olive oil
leaves of borage
sprig tarragon
handful each parsley and
mpernel

Cook the eggs in enough water to cover for 8 minutes, rinse briefly in cold water, peel and cool in cold water. • Peel the onion and slice into thin rings. Lay the onion rings in a salad bowl and sprinkle with salt. • Clean, rinse and tear apart the lettuce. Dry the lettuce or drain well. • Drain the tuna in a sieve. • Blend the vinegar, mustard, pepper, and oil in a bowl. Rinse and dry the borage, parsley, pimpernel, and tarragon, remove the tough stems, and chop. Add half of the herbs to the dressing. • Separate the tuna into pieces. Cut the eggs into eighths. Add both to the onion rings and dribble the dressing over them. Add the lettuce and other herbs. • Toss the lettuce once the salad is on the table. • Fresh French bread tastes great with this salad.

Greek Salad

Quick, easy to prepare

Preparation time: 20 minutes

| 2 tomatoes |
| 1 small cucumber |
| 1 green bell pepper |
| ½ lb. feta cheese |
| 1 red onion |
| 1 clove garlic |
| 3 tbs. red wine vinegar |
| 1 pinch mustard powder |
| ½ tsp. each salt and fresh coarsely ground black pepper |
| ½ tsp. dried oregano |
| 3 tbs. virgin olive oil |
| 2 oz. black olives |

Rinse, dry, and cut the tomatoes into eighths, removing the stem parts. • Rinse, dry and slice the cucumber (not too thin). • Halve the bell pepper, remove stem parts, ribs and seeds, rinse, dry and cut into strips. • Crumble the feta. • Peel the onion, slice into thin rings and combine with the cheese, bell pepper, cucumber, and tomatoes in a bowl. • Peel the garlic clove, crush and blend with the vinegar, mustard powder, salt, pepper and oregano. (Rub the oregano between your fingers when you add it). Add the olive oil bit by bit. • Pour the dressing over the salad and scatter the olives on top. • Oven-fresh garlic bread and Greek wine go well with this.

Tomato-Pepper Salad with Roast Beef

Quick, easy to prepare

Preparation time: 30 minutes

1 lb. green bell peppers
1 lb. tomatoes
1 handful spring onions
⅓ lb. sliced roast beef
2 hard-boiled eggs
3 tbs. red wine vinegar
½ tsp. each salt and freshly ground black pepper
½ tsp. sweet paprika powder
1 tsp. hot mustard
3 tbs. wheat seed oil
½ handful parsley

Halve the bell peppers, remove the stem parts, ribs, and seeds, rinse, dry and cut into strips. • Rinse, dry and slice the tomatoes. Remove any stem part • Trim, rinse, and slice the spring onions. • Cut the roast beef into strips. • Peel and slice the eggs. Combine all prepared ingredient in a salad bowl. • Blend the vinegar, salt, pepper, paprika, mustard and oil and toss with the salad. • Rinse and pat dry the parsley, remove tough stems, mince and sprinkle over the salad. Marinate the salad, covered, until time to serve. • Biscuits with butter taste great with this salad.

Tip: Yellow bell peppers are also quite tasty with this salad.

Asparagus and Ham Salad

Somewhat expensive

Preparation time: 40 minutes

lb. green asparagus
tsp. salt
eggs
lb. smoked ham
tbs. crème fraîche
tbs. fresh grapefruit juice
pinch each salt, white pepper
pinch sugar
tbs. chopped chives

Rinse the asparagus and dry. Thinly peel the lower, lighter parts, if needed, and cut off the woody ends. • Cut the asparagus into 2 inch pieces and put aside the tips. • Cook the asparagus pieces in enough salted water to cover for 15 minutes at low heat in a covered pot. Add the tips after 8 minutes of cooking. • Pierce the eggs at the large end, lay them into boiling water, and cook for 8 minutes. Rinse them in cold water, peel, allow to cool, and cut into eighths. • Remove the fatty rind of the ham and cut the ham into ½ inch wide strips. • Drain the asparagus in a sieve, reserving 1 tablespoon of the water. • Blend the crème fraîche with this tablespoon water, the grapefruit juice, salt, pepper, and sugar. • Arrange the asparagus, egg and ham on a platter and cover with the dressing and chives.

Pea and Egg Salad

Somewhat expensive

Preparation time: 30 minutes

1 lb. peas
½ tsp. salt
1 cup water
4 hard-boiled eggs
1 small head lettuce
4 tbs. fresh cheese (cottage or ricotta cheese)
2 tbs. mayonnaise
1 tbs. white wine vinegar
2 tbs. walnut oil
2 pinches each salt, sugar, and freshly ground white pepper
1 handful dill

Rinse the peas, pour them into a pot, add the salt and water and simmer the peas, covered, for about 15 minutes. • Peel the eggs and cut into eighths. • Discard any decayed leaves from the lettuce, separate the remaining leaves, rinse repeatedly and dry. Shred the lettuce. • Pour the cooked peas in a sieve and drain, saving 3 tablespoons of the cooking water. • Blend the fresh cheese with the mayonnaise, white wine vinegar, oil, salt, pepper, sugar, and enough of the water to make a thick dressing. Add the peas and shredded lettuce to the dressing and toss. • Arrange the egg on the salad. Rinse and dry the dill, remove the tough stems and chop the dill. Sprinkle it over the salad before serving.

Alexandre Dumas Salad

Famous recipe

Preparation time: 40 minutes

1 lb. young potatoes
2 eggs
½ lb. sweet and sour pickled red beets
¼ lb. wild greens
1 small cucumber
4 sardines canned in oil (boned)
1 tbs. red wine vinegar
3 tbs. dry red wine
1 pinch salt
1 pinch sugar
4 tsp. olive oil

Brush the potatoes well under running water. Bring to a boil in enough water to cover, and cook covered for 30 minutes. • Boil the eggs for 8 minutes, rinse briefly in cold water, peel and let cool. • Drain the beets and dice. • Rinse the wild greens several times, then drain. Rinse the cucumber, dry, and cut into strips. • Drain the sardines and separate into 1 inch pieces. • Pour off the potatoes, allow them to steam themselves dry, then peel and dice. • Slice the eggs. Arrange all ingredients on salad plates. • Blend the red wine vinegar, red wine, salt and sugar, then vigorously whisk in the oil. Pour the dressing over the salad evenly.

Avocado Salad with Watercress

Somewhat expensive

Preparation time: 25 minutes

2 eggs
1 handful watercress
3 avocados
15 black olives
4 anchovies
¼ lb. cream cheese
½ cup milk
1 tbs. olive oil
1 small onion
1 good pinch salt
1 pinch freshly ground black pepper

Pierce the eggs at the large end and lay them into boiling water to cook for 8 minutes. Rinse the eggs under cold water, then peel and allow to cool. • Rinse and drain the cress. Halve the avocadoes lengthwise and remove the seed. Cut up the avocadoes into inch cubes. • Halve and pit the olives. • Chop the anchovies. • Whisk together the cream cheese, milk and oil until they are of a creamy texture. • Peel and grate the onion. Combine the anchovies with the onion, salt, pepper, and dressing. • Cut the eggs into eighths. • Toss the avocado pieces and olives with the dressing. Arrange the salad, sprinkling the cress over it and garnishing with the eggs.

Green Bean Salad with Mozzarella

Easy to prepare, somewhat expensive

Preparation time: 45 minutes

| lb. young green beans
| sprigs summer savory
| tsp. salt
| lb. mozzarella cheese
| anchovies
| tbs. balsamic vinegar
| pinches each salt and freshly ground black pepper
| tbs. olive oil

Rinse and trim the beans, then cook them with the summer savory and salt in enough water to cover for 10 minutes. Pour the beans in a sieve, and let drain and cool. • Cut the mozzarella into small cubes. • Chop the anchovies. • Whisk together the vinegar, salt, pepper, chopped anchovies and olive oil until a smooth sauce results. • Put the cool beans and the cheese into a bowl, pour the dressing over them, and toss.

Tip: Mozzarella, an Italian cheese, was originally made in the Campagna region of Italy. It used to be made solely from buffalo milk. Today, the cheese is made of a blend of buffalo and regular milk, but some mozzarella is made the old-fashioned way, and it goes well with this recipe.

Seven Hills Bean Salad

Famous recipe

Preparation time: 40 minutes

| 1¼ lbs. young green beans |
| 1 handful fresh summer savory |
| ½ tsp. salt |
| 1 onion |
| 1 lb. small ripe tomatoes |
| 2 tbs. white wine vinegar |
| 2 pinches each salt and freshly ground black pepper |
| 1 pinch hot paprika powder |
| 1 tbs. sunflower seed oil |
| 2 oz. bacon |
| 2 tbs. freshly chopped parsley |

Rinse and trim the beans, halve the larger beans. Cook the beans with salt and summer savory in enough water to cover in a covered pot for 15 minutes over low heat. • Peel and chop the onion. • Rinse, dry, and cut the tomatoes into eighths, removing any stem parts. • Pour off the cooked beans and allow to cool. • Blend the wine vinegar with the salt, pepper, paprika, and oil. Toss the beans, onion, and tomatoes with the dressing and put aside, covered. • Fry the bacon until crispy, crumble it over the salad and toss, then sprinkle the parsley over the salad before serving.

Cheese Salad with Fruit

Nutritious, easy to prepare

Preparation time: 30 minutes

2 sour red apples (about ⅔ lb.)
⅓ lb. pickles
⅓ lb. Gouda cheese (not too young)
1 shallot
2 tbs. mayonnaise
2 tbs. each apple vinegar and sunflower seed oil
1 tsp. herbal salt
½ tsp. curry powder
1 pinch freshly ground white pepper
3 oz. cottage cheese (small curd)
2 seedless oranges
1 tbs. chopped chives

Rinse and dry the apples, then peel, quarter, core, and dice them. • Dice the pickles and the Gouda cheese. Peel and chop the shallot. • Blend the mayonnaise, vinegar, oil, salt, curry, and pepper. Combine the prepared ingredients, cottage cheese and dressing in a bowl and toss. • Peel the oranges and skin the segments. Toss the orange fillets and the chives with the salad.

Zucchini Salad with Ham

Somewhat expensive

Preparation time: 35 minutes

1 lb. zucchini
½ lb. chicory
⅔ lb. fresh pineapple
1 clementine orange
½ lb. smoked ham
3 tbs. fresh cheese (cottage cheese as substitute)
3 tbs. cream cheese
1 tbs. apple vinegar
1 tsp. lemon juice
2 tsp. maple syrup
1 pinch each salt, freshly ground white pepper, and paprika powder
½ bunch garden cress

Rub the zucchini well with a kitchen towel, rinse in lukewarm water, and dry. Cut in strips lengthwise and then dice the strips. • Discard outer, decayed leaves from the chicory, rinse and dry the stalks and cut out the wedge of bitter stem at the base. Cut the chicory into strips. • Remove the peel of the pineapple and the hard core. Cut the pineapple into evenly sized wedges. • Peel the clementine, divide into segments and halve these. • Remove any fatty rind from the ham and dice the slices of ham. • Combine the prepared ingredients in a salad bowl. • Blend the fresh cheese, cream cheese, apple vinegar, lemon juice, maple syrup, salt, pepper and paprika with a whisk. Add some water, if the dressing is too stiff. Gently toss the salad with the dressing. • Cut the leaves off the cress, rinse, drain and sprinkle them over the salad.

hef's Salad

mous recipe

eparation time: 30 minutes

bs. oil
lb. turkey breast
inch salt
inch freshly ground white pper
ggs
ead lettuce
lb. radicchio
cup sour cream
bs. mayonnaise
o 2 tbs. ketchup
sp. mustard
sp. lemon juice
inch sugar
mall onion
lb. Edam cheese
lb. cooked ham

eat the oil in a skillet. Sauté the rinsed and dried turkey the oil until browned on both des, about 5 minutes. Salt and epper to taste, and remove om skillet to cool. • Cook the ggs for 8 minutes, rinse in cold ater, peel and let cool in cold ater. • Discard decayed leaves d tough stems from the lettuce d radicchio, rinse and dry. • lend the sour cream with the ayonnaise, ketchup, mustard, mon juice and sugar. Peel and alve the onion, then crush it to the dressing. • Remove the nd from the cheese and cut to 2 inch strips, do the same ith the ham. Slice the eggs and rkey. • Arrange the lettuce and dicchio on a salad platter or ur plates. Arrange the turkey, am, cheese and eggs on the aves. Pour the dressing over e salad or offer it separately.

Oak Leaf Lettuce wit Chicken Livers

Inexpensive

Preparation time: 40 minutes

1 head oak leaf lettuce
1 lb. chicken livers
2 tbs. coconut oil
½ tsp. salt
1 pinch freshly ground white pepper
1 small clove garlic
1 pinch salt
1 tbs. apple vinegar
2 tbs. sunflower seed oil
2 tbs. freshly chopped parsley

Separate the oak leaf into leaves, rinse several times a dry. • Rinse and dry the livers, move any fatty deposits and ma an incision on the thicker side o each liver. • Heat the coconut c and sauté the livers on all sides; for about 3 minutes. Salt and p per to taste. • Peel the clove of garlic, crush it into a small bowl and blend with the salt, vinegar, and oil. • Tear the lettuce into 2 inch pieces and toss with the dressing. Arrange the lettuce on platter with the livers on top. • Sprinkle the parsley over the sal before serving.

Tip: Use endive, iceberg, or oth lettuce instead of oak leaf if de- sired.

Carpaccio Salad with Chicken Fillets

Easy to prepare

Preparation time: 45 minutes

boned and skinned chicken breasts

1 tsp. anise

1 piece of ginger root

1 tsp. salt

The "heart" of one stalk of celeriac

1 apple

1 small red bell pepper

slices fresh pineapple

2 tbs. wheat seed oil

salt and white pepper

Juice of 1 lemon

⅓ lb. crème fraîche

kiwis

attractive leaves of radicchio

Rinse the chicken and pat dry. • Chop the anise and grate about ½ teaspoon of the ginger root, then combine both with the salt. • Rub this mixture into the chicken and put it aside. • Wash the celeriac heart. Peel and core the apple. Halve the pepper, clean and rinse. Remove the peel from the pineapple slices. Dice the ingredients and combine. • Heat the oil and brown the chicken on each side for about 3 minutes. Salt and pepper each side after turning. • Blend the lemon juice, 1 pinch salt, 1 pinch pepper, and 1 pinch grated ginger, and the crème fraîche, then toss with the salad. • Peel and slice the kiwis. • Rinse the radicchio leaves and lay them on plates. Heap the salad on the leaves. • Slice the chicken thinly and arrange with the kiwi slices around the salad.

Carpaccio Salad with Devilfish

Somewhat expensive

Preparation time: 15 minutes
Marinating time: 1 hour
Final preparation: 30 minutes

| ½ lb. fillet of devilfish |
| 1 handful tarragon |
| 2 tsp. powdered green pepper |
| ⅓ lb. cherry tomatoes |
| 1 small cucumber |
| 2 shallots |
| ⅓ lb. mushrooms |
| 2 tbs. tarragon vinegar |
| 1 tsp. tarragon mustard |
| 3 tbs. grape seed oil |
| 1 good pinch each of sugar, salt, and freshly ground white pepper |
| A few nice lettuce leaves |

Rinse the fish fillet in cold water and pat dry. • Rinse the tarragon, dry and chop. Pulverize the green pepper. • Rub the tarragon and green pepper into the fish, wrap the fish in aluminum foil, and refrigerate for 1 hour. • Peel the tomatoes. • Peel and halve the cucumber, then scoop out the seeds with a spoon. Use a melon baller to make cucumber balls. • Peel and chop the shallots. Clean, rinse and slice the mushrooms. • Blend the vinegar, mustard, and oil, then toss with the salad. Add salt, pepper, and sugar to taste. • Rinse and dry the lettuce leaves, then lay them onto a platter. • Slice the fillet diagonally in very thin slices, arrange these around the outside of the platter and lightly salt them. Heap the mixed salad on the lettuce.

Chickpea Salad

Nutritious, inexpensive

Soaking time: 12 hours
Preparation time: 1 hour

½ lb. chickpeas
1 small bay leaf
1 head savoy cabbage (about 1 lb.)
1 tsp. salt
1 carrot (about ¼ lb.)
1 red onion
2 tbs. granulated vegetable bouillon
2 tbs. lemon juice
1 tbs. safflower seed oil
Some grated nutmeg
1 pinch black pepper
1 cup heavy cream
2 tbs. freshly chopped parsley

Soak the chickpeas overnight in 3 cups water. • Cook the chickpeas in the water with the bay leaf for 45 minutes, then drain in a sieve and remove the bay leaf. • While cooking the peas, remove any decayed leaves from the cabbage and quarter it. Remove the stem and shred the cabbage. Blanch the shredded cabbage in salted boiling water for 2 minutes and drain (or pour the drained cabbage into ice water to cool and then drain). • Wash, peel and coarsely grate the carrot. • Peel the onion, halve it lengthwise, and cut into thin slices. • Dissolve the vegetable bouillon in 2 tablespoons boiling water, then blend it with the lemon juice, oil, nutmeg and pepper. Toss the dressing with the salad. Marinate briefly. • Whip the cream half stiff and combine it and the parsley with the salad.

Oat Salad with Roquefort Dressing

Nutritious

Preparation time: 50 minutes
Marinating time: 10 minutes

3 cups water
1 tsp. sea salt
¼ tsp. each ground ginger and dried rosemary
⅓ lb. oats
1 cucumber (about 1 lb.)
¾ lb. ripe mango
2 oz. Roquefort cheese
2 tbs. each olive oil and sherry vinegar
3 to 4 tbs. cream
1 pinch black pepper
2 tbs. each freshly chopped dill and chive
2 to 3 oz. cashews

Bring the water with the salt, ginger, and rosemary to a boil, then scatter in the oats and cook the kernels until they are soft (35 to 50 minutes, depending on the size of the kernels). Drain and let cool in a sieve. • Wash, dry and dice the cucumber. • Peel and pit the mango and dice it. • With a fork, mash the cheese in a large flat bowl and blend in the oil and vinegar. Add the cream and pepper and whip this into a velvety dressing. • Toss the dressing and the herbs with the prepared ingredients. Marinate for about 10 minutes. Toss the cashews with the salad before serving.

Millet Vegetable Salad

Nutritious, easy to prepare

Preparation time: 45 minutes

⅓ lb. millet

1 to 2 tsp. salt

2 cups vegetable bouillon

⅓ lb. carrots

⅓ lb. red beets

1 large tart apple

2 tbs. lemon juice

½ lb. yogurt

1 pinch each salt and freshly ground black pepper

1 dash Tabasco sauce

½ bunch garden cress

2 tbs. sesame seeds

Sprinkle the millet and salt into the boiling vegetable bouillon. Cook, covered, over low heat for 20 minutes, then let cool. • Peel and coarsely grate the carrots and red beets. • Peel, halve and core the apple. Thinly slice the apple halves and sprinkle the lemon juice over it. Combine the vegetables and apples and arrange on 4 plates. • Heap the cooled millet on the vegetable-apple mixture. • Blend the yogurt, salt, pepper and Tabasco sauce. Pick the leaves off the cress, rinse them in a sieve, dry and combine with the dressing. Pour the dressing over the millet. Toast the sesame seeds in an ungreased pan and then sprinkle them over the salad.

Viper's Grass Root Salad with Beef

Needs some time

Preparation time: 1 hour
Marinating time: 30 minutes

2 tbs. vinegar

2 tbs. flour

1 lb. viper's grass root

1 pint beef broth

2 carrots

½ lb. frozen peas

1 lb. cooked, lean beef

4 tbs. herbal vinegar

1 tsp. salt

½ tsp. each freshly ground black pepper and sweet paprika

1 tsp. mustard

4 tbs. wheat seed oil

2 tbs. freshly chopped parsley

Stir the flour and vinegar into 1 quart water in a bowl. Rinse and thinly peel the viper's grass root, dice and immediately put the pieces into the water to avoid discoloration. • Cook the roots in the beef broth for 25 to 30 minutes. • Rinse, peel and slice the carrots and add them to the cooking root 10 minutes before it is done. • Bring the peas to a boil in ½ cup water and cook for 5 minutes. • Cube the meat. • Pour off the water from the root and carrots, reserving ½ cup of the water. Drain the peas in a sieve and combine them with the other vegetables and the beef. • Blend the reserved broth with the vinegar, salt, pepper, paprika powder, and mustard. Whisk in the oil and add the parsley. • Toss the salad with the warm dressing and marinate, covered, for 30 minutes.

Tomato-Pepper Salad with Wheat

Easy to prepare, inexpensive

Soaking time: 12 hours
Preparation time: 30 minutes
Marinating time: 30 minutes

⅓ lb. wheat	
1 green pepper	
½ lb. tomatoes	
3 tbs. apple vinegar	
1 pinch each salt and freshly ground white pepper	
1 pinch sugar	
⅛ tsp. mustard	
½ tsp. sweet paprika	
3 tbs. safflower seed oil	
1 clove garlic	
1 small onion	
1 handful dill	
1 handful chives	

Rinse the wheat kernels under running water and soak them overnight in ½ quart water. Cook the wheat the next day in the soaking water for 20 minutes. • Rinse and halve the pepper, remove all stems, ribs and seeds, then cut into strips. • Peel the tomatoes, then cut them into eighths, removing any stem parts. • Combine these ingredients. • Blend the vinegar, salt, pepper, sugar, mustard, paprika powder, and oil. Peel the garlic clove and onion. Crush the garlic into the dressing, finely chop the onion and add it to the dressing, as well. • Rinse, drain, and chop the herbs, then add them to the dressing. • Pour the dressing over the salad. Toss well and marinate for 30 minutes.

Green Rye with Horseradish Dressing

Takes some time

Soaking time: 12 hours
Preparation time: 30 minutes
Marinating time: 30 minutes

¼ lb. green rye	
½ quart water	
½ tsp. salt	
1 firm ripe pear	
2 tbs. lemon juice	
½ cucumber	
1 green and 1 red bell pepper	
¼ lb. yogurt	
2 tbs. crème fraîche	
2 tbs. horseradish (from a jar)	
2 tbs. apple vinegar	
2 pinches each salt and white pepper	
1 pinch sugar	
1 bunch cress	

Rinse the green rye well under running water, then soak it overnight in ½ quart water. • The next day, cook the rye in its soaking water plus the salt for 20 minutes over low heat, then drain in a sieve. • Wash the pear well, dry, halve, core and cut the fruit into strips. Dribble the lemon juice over the fruit to avoid discoloration. • Rinse, dry and slice the cucumber. • Rinse and dry the peppers, halve, then remove all seeds, rib and stem parts. Cut the pepper halves into thin strips. • Blend the yogurt, crème fraîche, horseradish, apple vinegar, salt, pepper, and sugar. Toss well with the salad, then marinate for 30 minutes. Garnish with the garden cress.

entil Sprout Salad

asy to prepare, somewhat
xpensive

eparation time: 40 minutes
arinating time: 30 minutes

lb. lentil sprouts
medium red onions
head chicory
head endive or romaine lettuce
pink grapefruit
tbs. almonds
lb. crème fraîche
to 2 tbs. horseradish
pinches each salt and freshly
ound white pepper
to 5 tbs. (fruit based) vinegar
spring onions
hard-boiled eggs

R inse the sprouts, blanch
them in a sieve in boiling
ater for 5 minutes, then drain.
Peel and dice the onions. Re-
ove the outer, decayed leaves
om the chicory, rinse and make
wedge shaped incision in the
em to cut out the bitter end.
ut the stalk into rings. •
eparate the leaves of the endive
lettuce, rinse them and shred.
Halve the grapefruit and cut
ut the segments with a sharp
nife. • Coarsely chop the al-
onds. • Combine all ingre-
ents. • Press the juice remain-
g in the grapefruit halves into
is mixture. • Blend the crème
aîche, horseradish, salt, pepper,
nd vinegar. Clean the spring
nions, slice into rings, and add
the dressing. Pour the dressing
ver the salad, toss, and allow to
arinate for 30 minutes. • Peel
nd cut the eggs into eighths,
en garnish the salad with them.

Caponata

Famous recipe, takes som time

Preparation time: 1½ hours
Cooling time: 2 hours

1 lb. eggplant
1 tsp. salt
2 tbs. raisins
½ lb. onions
½ lb. tomatoes
1 small celery stalk
2 oz. green olives
6 tbs. olive oil
1 tbs. capers
1 tbs. pine nuts
1 pinch each salt and freshly ground black pepper
½ cup mild wine vinegar
1 tbs. sugar

Cut off the stem parts of the eggplant. Rinse the eggplant, dice and sprinkle the salt over the pieces. Let stand for 3 minutes. • Rinse the raisins in warm water and drain in a sieve • Peel the onions and cut into thin rings. • Parboil the tomatoes, peel, and remove ste parts and seeds. Chop the tomatoes. • Wash the celery. C the stalk into 1 inch pieces, blanch for 5 minutes in a little boiling water, and drain. • Pit th olives and coarsely chop. • Rins off the eggplant pieces, press ou the moisture and pat dry. • Hea 4 tablespoons oil and brown th eggplant for a few minutes over high heat. Take out the eggplan add 2 tablespoons oil to the sk let and reduce the heat. Sauté the onion rings until they are translucent. Sauté the celery pieces briefly together with the onions, then add the tomatoes. Five minutes later, add the olive capers, raisins, pine nuts and th eggplant. • Add salt, pepper, sugar and vinegar to taste, cook the vegetables together another 10 minutes, allowing the vinega to steam off. Serve the caponat after it has cooled.

...lad with White ...ans

...y to prepare, inexpensive

...king time: 8 to 12 hours
...aration time: 70 minutes
...inating time: 1 hour

...b. white beans
...ps water
...sp. salt
...b. soybean sprouts
...d apple
...e of ½ lemon
...cucumber
...ennel bulb
...ttle over ½ lb. lean cooked
...
...s. herbal vinegar
...s. grated horseradish
...nches each salt and freshly
...und white pepper
... 4 tbs. sunflower seed oil
...s. coarsely chopped walnuts

Soak the beans overnight in plenty of water. • Cook the beans in fresh water for 1 hour, over low heat. Add the salt only after 50 minutes. • Blanch the sprouts 3 minutes in boiling water and drain. • Wash, quarter and core the apple. Slice the quarters thinly and sprinkle lemon juice over the apple to avoid discoloration. • Peel and cut the cucumber into thin strips. • Discard the outer leaves of the fennel and trim the stems. Wash the halves of the bulb and cut into strips. • Likewise, cut the ham into thin strips. • Combine all ingredients. • Drain the beans and add to the rest of the vegetables while still warm. • Blend the vinegar, horseradish, salt, pepper and oil for a dressing. Toss this dressing with the walnuts and the salad and marinate for 1 hour.

Salad with Black Beans

Quick, easy to prepare

Soaking time: 12 hours
Preparation time: 1¼ hours
Marinating time: 1 hour

½ lb. black beans
3 sprigs summer savory
½ tsp. salt
2 to 3 tbs. orange juice
4 tbs. vinegar
1 pinch each salt and cayenne pepper
4 tbs. oil
1 handful parsley
1 large onion (about ½ lb.)
2 medium oranges

Wash the beans and soak them overnight in cold water. • Pour off the soaking water and cook the beans and two sprigs of summer savory in 3 cups water for 1 hour. Add the salt only after the beans have cooked for 50 minutes. • Blend the orange juice with the vinegar, salt, cayenne pepper, and oil. Rinse the parsley, dry, chop with the remaining savory, and add to the dressing. • Drain the beans. Pour the dressing over the beans while they are still hot. • Peel and chop the onion, toss with the beans and marinate for 1 hour. • Peel the oranges. Slice the oranges and arrange the slices on a platter, then heap the bean salad on them.

Lentil Salad with Country Cooked Ham

Easy to prepare

Preparation time: 30 minutes

½ lb. red lentils
1 small onion
½ lb. smoked country ham, cooked
2 kiwis
1 tbs. lemon juice
2 pinches salt
1 pinch each sugar and freshly ground white pepper
2 tsp. maple syrup
1 tbs. sunflower seed oil
2 tbs. chopped chives

Put the lentils in a pot with enough water to cover. Peel and halve the onion, add it to the pot and bring everything to a boil, covered. Cook the lentils over low heat for 15 to 20 minutes. • Finely dice the ham. • Peel and quarter the kiwis, then slice the quarters. • Blend the lemon juice, salt, pepper, and sugar. Add the maple syrup and whisk in the oil. • Drain the lentils in a sieve and allow to cool. • Gently toss the lentils with the ham and kiwis, then add the dressing. Spice to taste for a definite sweet-and-sour flavor. • Sprinkle the chives over the salad before serving.

Ham Salad

Somewhat expensive

Preparation time: 30 minutes

½ lb. frozen peas
1 pinch salt
4 tbs. water
Just under 1 lb. ham, without any fatty rind
1 large pickle
¼ lb. wild greens
2 tsp. lemon juice
1 pinch each salt and freshly ground black pepper
2 tbs. corn oil
10 oz. canned corn
2 tbs. pearl onions (from a jar)

Pour the frozen peas into the boiling, salted water and cook, covered, over low heat, for 3 minutes. Then drain the peas in a sieve. Reserve 1 tablespoon of the cooking water. • Cut the ham into strips ½ inch wide and 1½ inches long. Cut the pickle the same way. • Trim the stems of the wild greens, rinse the greens several times and dry. Blend the lemon juice with the salt, pepper, and reserved broth. Whisk in the oil, then toss the dressing with the wild greens. Gently toss this with the ham, pickle, peas, corn, and pearl onions.

Tip: Substitute chicory or endive for the field salad if desired.

Beef Salad with Red Beets

Easy to prepare, inexpensive

Preparation time: 30 minutes
Marinating time: 2 hours

1 lb. lean beef, cooked
5-6 oz. pickled red beets
1 large pickle
2 onions
4 oz. canned corn
3 tbs. red wine vinegar
1 tbs. juice from beets
2 pinches each salt and freshly ground black pepper
1 tsp. mustard
2 tbs. freshly chopped herbs: marjoram, parsley, chives, basil
4 tbs. oil

Thinly slice the beef. • Dice the beets and pickle. • Peel the onions and slice them into thin rings. Drain the corn. • Blend the red wine vinegar, beet juice, salt, pepper, mustard, herbs and oil. • Put all ingredients in a bowl, toss with the dressing, and marinate for at least 2 hours.

Bean and Beef Salad

Inexpensive, easy to prepare

Preparation time: 45 minutes

1 lb. green beans
1 quart water
½ tsp. salt
1 lb. lean beef, cooked
1 large white onion
2 tomatoes
2 hard-boiled eggs
4 tbs. mayonnaise
2 tbs. ketchup
⅓ lb. sour cream
1 tbs. red wine vinegar
1 pinch each salt and freshly ground black pepper
1 pinch sugar
1 small head Boston lettuce
2 tbs. freshly chopped parsley

Clean, rinse and cut the beans into pieces. Cook them in the salted water for 20 minutes. • Cut the beef into strips. • Peel and chop the onion. • Rinse, dry and cut the tomatoes into eighths. • Peel and quarter the eggs. • Blend the mayonnaise with the ketchup, sour cream, vinegar, salt, pepper, and sugar. • Separate the leaves of the lettuce, rinse, dry, and lay out in a salad bowl. • Drain the beans, allow them to cool a little, then combine them with the strips of meat, onion and tomatoes. Pour the dressing over this and toss. Heap the salad on the lettuce leaves. • Garnish with the eggs and parsley.

Tip: Use leftovers from a roast for this recipe.

Rice Salad with Yogurt Dressing

Easy to prepare, quick

Preparation time: 30 minutes
Marinating time: 30 minutes

1 cup chicken broth
½ lb. fillet of chicken breast
½ qt. water
½ tsp. salt
¼ lb. long grain rice
4 mandarin oranges
5 oz. yogurt
2 tbs. mayonnaise
3 tbs. lemon juice
2 tbs. soy sauce
1 tsp. curry powder
1 pinch white pepper
2 tbs. raisins
2 bananas

Bring the chicken broth to a boil. • Lay the chicken in the broth and cook, covered, over low heat for 20 minutes. • Bring the salted water to a boil in a pot. Pour in the rice, stir once and cook, uncovered, for 15 minutes over medium heat. • Peel 2 mandarin oranges and divide into segments. Juice the other 2 mandarin oranges. • Blend the orange juice with the yogurt, mayonnaise, lemon juice, soy sauce, curry powder, and pepper. • Rinse the raisins and add them to the rice for the last 5 minutes of cooking. • Rinse the rice in a sieve and drain. • Dice the chicken. • Blend 6 tablespoons of the broth with the dressing in a salad bowl. • Peel and slice the bananas and toss them with all the other ingredients. • Marinate, covered, for 30 minutes.

Spanish Rice Salad

Somewhat more expensive

Preparation time: 45 minutes
Serves: 6 people

½ lb. long grain rice
½ tsp. salt
2 green bell peppers
1 lb. tomatoes
½ grilled chicken
½ lb. small shrimp, cooked
1 can of tuna fish
2 onions
¼ lb. black olives
6 tbs. red wine vinegar
½ tsp. each salt and freshly ground black pepper
½ tsp. sweet paprika
4 tbs. virgin olive oil
4 anchovy fillets
2 tbs. freshly chopped parsley

Sprinkle the rice into a little more than 2 cups of boiling salted water and cook for 15 minutes over low heat. • Halve the peppers, rinse, clean, and cut them into strips. • Rinse and cut the tomatoes into eighths, removing any stem parts. • Bone and skin the chicken and dice the meat. • Rinse and drain the shrimp. Drain the tuna well and separate the chunks. • Peel and chop the onion. • Pit the olives. • Drain the rice in a sieve and allow to cool somewhat, then combine it with the other ingredients. • Blend the vinegar with the salt, pepper, paprika, and oil. Pat dry the anchovy fillets, chop and crush, then blend with the sauce. Toss the salad with the dressing and sprinkle the parsley over it before serving.

Broccoli-Asparagus Salad

Somewhat expensive

Preparation time: 40 minutes
Serves: 6 people

2 lbs. asparagus
1 tsp. salt
2 lbs. broccoli
1 tbs. granulated chicken broth
1 lb. smoked salmon
1 tbs. mustard
½ tsp each salt and freshly ground white pepper
2 tsp. dry sherry
1 tbs. maple syrup
3 tbs. white wine vinegar
2 egg yolks
½ cup wheat seed oil
1 handful dill

Thinly peel the asparagus from top to bottom, bundle with kitchen twine and cook in 1 quart boiling water with ½ teaspoon salt for 15 to 20 minutes. • Trim the broccoli, cut into pieces and cook with ½ teaspoon salt and the chicken broth in 1 quart water for 15 minutes. • Cut the salmon into broad strips. • Blend the mustard with the salt, pepper, sherry, maple syrup and vinegar. Blend in the egg yolks and whisk in the oil in a thin stream. • Rinse, dry, and mince the dill, then add it to the dressing. • Take the asparagus from the water and use only the top third of each stalk for the salad. • Drain the broccoli in a sieve, reserving ½ cup of the broth. • Halve the asparagus pieces and arrange with the salmon and broccoli on a platter. Add salt, pepper, and vinegar to the dressing to taste and then pour it over the salad. • Serve the mustard sauce separately.

Smoked Fish Salad

Easy to prepare, quick

Preparation time: 30 minutes

4 eggs
1 head endive
4 tomatoes
¼ lb. mushrooms
2 tbs. lemon juice
1 small fresh chili pepper
1 pinch salt
2 tbs. wine vinegar
5 tbs. olive oil
1 lb. smoked shark fillet
10 black olives

Cook the eggs in boiling water for 8 minutes, rinse briefly under cold water, peel, and cool in cold water. • Discard decayed leaves and tough stems from the endive, shred, rinse several times (it is often quite sandy), and dry or drain well. • Rinse the tomatoes and cut out the stem parts. Then cut the tomatoes into eighths. • Clean and rinse the mushrooms, then thinly slice them and put them in a salad bowl. Pour the lemon juice over them and carefully toss with the mushrooms. • Halve the chili pepper, remove the stem and seeds. Rinse the pepper, slice into thin strips and sprinkle some salt over it in a bowl. Add the vinegar and vigorously blend in the oil. • Slice the shark, cut the eggs into eighths, and drain the olives. • Add the tomatoes, shark, eggs, olives, and the dressing to the mushrooms. Add the endive, but do not toss until the salad is on the table. • Rolls go well with this dish.

Party
Salads

New or old-fashioned, they are always a success.
They stimulate curiosity and pleasure
and they give a strong foundation
to an evening of good cheer.

Fine Herring Salad

Takes some time, easy to prepare

Soaking time: 30 minutes
Preparation time: 40 minutes
Marinating time: 2 hours
Serves: 8 people

8 salted herring with the milt
5 eggs
4 tbs. cream
8 tbs. lemon juice
1 tbs. mustard
½ cup sunflower seed oil
1 pinch freshly ground black pepper
½ tsp. sugar
4 tbs. capers
2 onions
4 small cucumbers
1 lb. pickled red beets
1 lb. pork roast, sliced
½ handful parsley

Skin and bone the herring. Take out the milt. Soak the herring fillet and the milt for 30 minutes in cold water. Change the water once, after about 15 minutes. • Cook the eggs in boiling water for about 8 minutes, rinse briefly under cold water, and peel. • Strain the yolks of 4 eggs and the milt through a sieve. Vigorously blend in the cream, lemon juice, mustard and oil. Add the pepper, sugar and capers to this sauce. • Peel and chop the onions. Dice the cucumbers, the whites of 4 eggs, beets, pork, and herring fillets. Toss these with the sauce and marinate, covered, for 2 hours. • Cut the remaining egg into eighths and garnish the salad with the egg and the parsley.

Chicken and Rice Salad

Takes some time

Preparation time: 2 hours
Marinating time: 1 hour
Serves: 8 people

1 chicken (about 3 lbs.)
2 qts. water
1½ tsp. salt
1 handful soup herbs (a bundle of 1 carrot, parsley root, a piece of celeriac, and a piece of leek)
½ tsp. peppercorns
½ lb. long grain rice
½ lb. mayonnaise
8 tbs. condensed milk
2 tsp. mustard
8 tbs. lemon juice
2 tbs. soy sauce
3 tsp. curry powder
1 pinch powdered ginger
1 tsp. sugar
1 clove garlic
4 mandarin oranges
2 apples
¼ lb. mushrooms
1 tbs. butter

Cook the chicken in 1 quart water with 1 teaspoon salt for 1½ to 2 hours. • Add the soup herbs and peppercorns to the broth after 1 hour of cooking. • Cook the rice in 1 quart water with ½ teaspoon salt for 12 minutes, then drain. • Blend the mayonnaise with the condensed milk, mustard, lemon juice, soy sauce, curry, ginger, sugar, and the crushed garlic. • Peel the mandarin oranges and the apples, segment or slice and add to the dressing with the rice. • Clean and rinse the mushrooms, slice them, and sauté the slices in the butter. • Dice the chicken and add to the salad with the mushrooms. Marinate, covered, for 1 hour.

Flemish Salad

Famous Recipe

Soaking time: 4 hours
Preparation time: 1 hour
Serves: 8 people

1¼ lbs. salted herring

½ quart milk

4 lbs. potatoes (should stay firm after cooking)

4 medium onions

3 tbs. coconut oil

4 heads chicory

3 to 4 tbs. white wine vinegar

6 tbs. wheat seed oil

1 handful each chervil and tarragon

Soak the herring in enough water to cover for 3 hours. Refresh the water 3 times during this period. Pour off this water, and soak the herring in the milk for 1 hour. • Brush the potatoes well under running water. Bring to a boil in enough water to cover and cook for about 30 minutes. • Peel and chop the onions. • Heat the coconut oil in a pan and brown the onions until golden. Drain the onions on a paper towel. • Remove the outer chicory leaves, rinse and dry the rest. Cut out the bitter wedge from the stem. Cut the chicory into strips, but not too thin. • Remove the herring from the milk, pat dry, and cut into equally sized pieces. • Drain the potatoes, let them steam dry, peel, and cut them into strips. • Combine the herring pieces, potatoes, onions, and chicory with the white wine vinegar and the wheat seed oil, adjust to taste. Allow to marinate briefly. • Rinse, dry, and chop the chervil and tarragon. Sprinkle the herbs over the salad.

Potato Bean Salad

Takes some time

Preparation time: 1 hour
Marinating time: 1 hour
Serves: 8 people

4 lbs. potatoes (should stay firm after cooking)
1 lb. green beans
1 handful summer savory
2 pinches salt
1 clove garlic
2 medium onions
1 bunch thyme
1 pinch freshly ground white pepper
½ cup hot beef broth
½ cup wine vinegar
2 tsp. mustard
1 pinch sugar
8 medium tomatoes
1 lb. feta cheese
¼ lb. stuffed olives
2 oz. black olives
1 handful each parsley and basil
4 tbs. each sunflower seed oil and olive oil

Rinse the potatoes. Cook for 20 minutes in enough water to cover. • Clean, trim, halve the beans. Cook the beans, covered, with the summer savory and a pinch of salt in ½ cup water for 15 minutes, then drain. • Drain the potatoes, peel, then halve or quarter. Rub the inside of a salad bowl with the split garlic clove. In this bowl, combine the potatoes, beans, peeled and chopped onions, thyme, a pinch of salt and pepper. • Blend the broth with the vinegar, mustard and sugar, pour this over the other ingredients, and toss well. • Marinate for 1 hour. • Cut the tomatoes into eighths, dice the feta cheese, rinse and chop the herbs. • Add all these with the olives and the oil to the salad, and toss well.

Brown Rice Salad with Vegetables

Inexpensive, easy to prepare

Preparation time: 50 minutes
Marinating time: 15 minutes
Serves: 8 people

1 lb. brown rice	
1 quart water	
½ tsp. salt	
3 carrots	
3 stalks leek	
1 lb. celeriac (knob celery)	
¼ lb. chopped walnuts	
4 tbs. herbal vinegar	
2 tbs. lemon juice	
2 pinches each salt and freshly ground white pepper	
3 tbs. walnut oil	
3 tbs. freshly chopped parsley	

Pour the rice into the boiling salted water and cook for 30 minutes over low heat, then pour into a sieve and drain. • Peel, rinse and julienne the carrots. • Remove the root ends and greens from the leeks, halve the stalks, rinse well, and slice thinly. • Peel the celeriac, cut into thin strips, and combine with the walnuts, leek, carrots, and cooked rice. • Blend the vinegar, lemon juice, salt, pepper, oil, and chopped parsley, then toss with the salad. • Marinate, covered, for 15 minutes.

Rice Salad with Cucumber and Mushrooms

Inexpensive, easy to prepare

Preparation time: 40 minutes
Marinating time: 15 minutes
Serves: 8 people

1 lb. long grain rice	
1 quart water	
½ tsp. salt	
1 lb. mushrooms	
1 cucumber	
2 onions	
⅓ lb. ham	
2 tbs. small capers	
5 tbs. herbal vinegar	
1 tsp. each salt and freshly ground black pepper	
5 tbs. olive oil	
2 handfuls mixed herbs (chervil, chives and tarragon)	

Pour the rice into the boiling, salted water, and cook for 20 minutes over low heat, then drain in a sieve. • Clean, rinse and thinly slice the mushrooms. • Rinse the cucumber in lukewarm water, dry, and slice. • Peel and chop the onions. Cut the ham into thin strips.. Drain the capers. • Combine the cooled rice with the prepared ingredients. • Blend the vinegar, salt, and pepper, then whisk in the oil. Rinse and dry the herbs, then finely chop. Toss the herbs, dressing and salad.

Lentil and Brown Rice Salad

Easy to prepare

Soaking time: 1 hour
Preparation time: 50 minutes
Marinating time: 20 minutes
Serves: 8 people

½ lb. each lentils and brown rice

1 tbs. granulated vegetable bouillon

1 bay leaf

2 tsp. dried thyme

2 large onions

6 tbs. olive oil

2 apples

Just under ½ lb. pickles

1 lb. cooked beef

2 cups sour cream

2 tbs. each soy sauce, apple vinegar, and capers

1 oz. anchovy fillets

2 to 3 pinches freshly ground black pepper

3 tbs. freshly chopped parsley

⅓ to ¾ cup liquid from the pickles

Soak the lentils for 1 hour in 1 quart water. • Cook the lentils and the rice with the vegetable bouillon, bay leaf, and dried thyme in the soaking water for 40 minutes. Drain and remove the bay leaf. • Peel and chop the onions, then lightly brown in the olive oil. • Rinse, quarter, core and dice the apples. • Dice the pickles. • Cut the beef into thin strips. • Blend the sour cream with the soy sauce and vinegar. Chop the capers and anchovy, toss these, and the herbs, with the salad and dressing, then pepper to taste. • Marinate for 20 minutes. Add the parsley, then add enough liquid from the pickles to get a moist salad.

Green Rye and Rye Salad

Nutritious, inexpensive

Soaking time: 12 hours
Preparation time: 50 minutes
Marinating time: 30 minutes
Serves: 8 people

¼ lb. each green rye and rye

1 quart water

1 tbs. granulated vegetable bouillon

1 lb. green beans

¾ lb. leek

⅓ lb. stuffed olives

6 tbs. each olive oil, vinegar, and tomato paste

2 tsp. chopped basil

1 tsp. ground coriander

2 to 3 pinches freshly ground black pepper

2 tbs. freshly chopped parsley

Bring the rye kernels and bouillon to a boil, then remove from heat and soak, covered, for 12 hours. • Cook the kernels in their soaking water for about 40 minutes. • Clean, rinse, and halve the beans, then cook them with the kernels for the last 20 minutes. • Drain the beans and kernels. • Blend the oil, vinegar, and tomato paste, and combine with the prepared ingredients, along with the leeks and stuffed olives. Add basil, coriander, and pepper to taste, then marinate for 30 minutes. Add the parsley before serving.

Onion Salad

Balkan Specialty

Preparation time: 50 minutes
Serves: 8 people

2 lbs. red and white onions
4 cloves garlic
1 tsp. salt
5 tbs. red wine vinegar
½ tsp. each sugar and freshly ground black pepper
3 tbs. olive oil
8 leaves of wild garlic
4 slices of whole-wheat bread
2 tbs. butter

Peel the onions and the garlic, then slice into very thin rings. Sprinkle the salt over them and let stand, covered, for 30 minutes. • Blend the vinegar, pepper and sugar. Whisk in the oil. • Rinse and dry the wild garlic leaves, then cut into thin strips. • Toss the onions and dressing well and sprinkle the wild garlic over the salad. • Toast the bread and dice. Brown the bread in the butter and scatter over the salad.

Tofu Salad with Beans

Nutritious recipe

Preparation time: 45 minutes
Marinating time: 1 hour
Serves: 8 people

1 lb. tofu
2 tbs. soy sauce
2 pinches freshly ground black pepper
1 lb. green beans
⅔ lb. green bell peppers
½ lb. mushrooms
3 tbs. sunflower seed oil
¼ lb. cream
3 tbs. white wine vinegar
1 tbs. Worcestershire sauce
1 tsp. sweet paprika powder
2 tsp. freshly chopped or 1 tsp. dried and crumbled basil
2 shallots
1 lb. tomatoes
3 tbs. crème fraîche
2 tbs. each freshly chopped parsley and chives

Slice the tofu into approximately 1 inch cubes and marinate with the soy sauce and 1 pinch pepper. • Clean, trim, and rinse the beans, then cook them in enough water to cover for 20 minutes. • Rinse, and quarter the bell peppers, remove all stem parts, ribs and seeds, then cut into thin strips. Cook these with the beans for the last 2 or 3 minutes. Drain the vegetables. • Clean, rinse and thinly slice the mushrooms. Heat the oil in a skillet, and add the tofu with its marinade. Sauté the tofu for 5 minutes. Add the mushrooms, and sauté for another 3 to 4 minutes. Pour in the cream and sprinkle some pepper over the mixture. Cover and cook for another 5 minutes. • Combine the prepared ingredients with the vinegar, Worcestershire sauce, paprika powder, and basil. • Marinate for 1 hour. • Peel the shallots and slice into thin rings. Rinse the tomatoes and dice. Toss these with the crème fraîche, herbs and salad.

Cheese Salad with Shrimp

Quick, slightly expensive

Preparation time: 30 minutes
Marinating time: 1 hour

1 lb. aged Gouda	
3 firm, ripe pears	
2 tsp. lemon juice	
½ lb. cooked small shrimp	
¼ lb. yogurt	
1 tbs. safflower seed oil	
3 tbs. lemon juice	
3 tbs. crème fraîche	
2 tsp. mustard	
2 pinches salt	
2 pinches freshly ground white pepper	
1 handful chives	
½ head Boston lettuce	

Slice the cheese, then cut the slices into strips. • Rinse, dry, halve and core the pears. Dice the pears and sprinkle the lemon juice over them right away to avoid discoloration. • Rinse and drain the shrimp, then add them to the other salad ingredients. • Blend the yogurt, oil, lemon juice, crème fraîche and mustard. Salt and pepper to taste. Rinse and dry the chives, mince and add to the dressing. • Pour the dressing over the salad, toss lightly and marinate, covered, in a cool place for at least 1 hour. • Rinse and dry the lettuce leaves, then lay them out in a large salad bowl. Heap the cheese salad on the lettuce.

Serbian Salad

Quick, easy to prepare

Preparation time: 40 minutes
Serves: 8 people

1 lb. mayonnaise	
4 tbs. lemon juice	
2 tsp. mustard	
½ tsp. sugar	
1 tsp. sweet paprika powder	
1 pinch white pepper	
1 lb. pickles	
2 red bell peppers	
6 apples	
6 bananas	
1 head iceberg lettuce	

Blend the mayonnaise with the lemon juice and mustard. Add sugar, paprika, and pepper to taste. • Julienne the pickles. Halve the bell peppers, remove all stem parts, ribs and seeds, then rinse. Cut the peppers into thin strips and combine with the pickles and dressing. • Peel, quarter and core the apples. Make thick slices, then cut the apple into strips and add to the salad. Peel and halve the bananas lengthwise, then slice and add to the salad. • Separate the leaves of lettuce, tear into bite-size pieces, rinse, and dry. Lay the lettuce in a salad bowl or platter and arrange the salad on it.

Curry-Rice Salad with Mango

Takes some time

Preparation time: 1 hour and 20 minutes
Marinating time: 2 hours
Serves: 8 people

1 large chicken (3 lbs.)
1 handful soup herbs (a bundle of 1 carrot, parsley root, a piece of celeriac, and a piece of leek)
1½ qts. water
1 tsp. salt
1 tsp. white peppercorns
1 bay leaf
2 lemons
3 tsp. curry powder
¼ lb. long grain rice
5 tbs. mayonnaise
2 tbs. sherry vinegar
2 tbs. crème fraîche
1 pinch white pepper
½ tsp. chopped lemon balm
3 to 4 ripe mangoes
2 or 3 sprigs lemon balm

Rinse the chicken. Rinse and coarsely chop the soup herbs. Bring the salted water to a boil. Cook the chicken, peppercorns, soup greens, and bay leaf for 45 minutes. • Remove the chicken from the broth and allow to cool. • Pour the broth through a sieve and bring to a boil again. Rinse the lemons well, slice thinly, and add them, together with the curry powder and the rice, to the broth. Cook for 20 to 25 minutes. • While waiting for the rice, skin and bone the chicken and dice the meat. • Drain the rice well in a sieve. • Blend the mayonnaise, vinegar, crème fraîche, pepper, and lemon balm. Combine the rice, chicken, and dressing. • Marinate for 2 hours. • Peel the mangoes, dice, and toss with the salad. Garnish with the sprigs of lemon balm.

Bean Salad with Apples

Specialty from Russia

Soaking time: 12 hours
Preparation time: 1½ hours
Standing time: 30 minutes
Final preparation: 35 minutes
Serves: 8 people

1 lb. white (navy) beans
1½ qts. water
1 tsp. salt
Juice of 1 lemon
2 tsp. Dijon mustard
4 tbs. crème fraîche
½ tsp. each salt, sugar, ground black pepper, and dried, crumbled marjoram
3 shallots
2 sweet and sour pickles
2 large tart apples
4 hard-boiled eggs

Rinse the beans and soak in the water. • The next day, bring the beans to a boil in their soaking water and cook for 1½ hours, adding the salt only in the last minutes of cooking. Blend the lemon juice with the mustard, crème fraîche, salt, pepper, sugar and marjoram. • Drain the beans and toss with the dressing while still warm. • Marinate for 30 minutes. • Peel and chop the shallots. Dice the pickles. • Peel, quarter, core and dice the apples. • Peel and chop the hard-boiled eggs. • Add the shallots, pickles, and apples to the beans and toss well. • Sprinkle the chopped eggs over the salad before serving.

White Bean and Tomato Salad

Easy to prepare, inexpensive

Soaking time: 12 hours
Preparation time: 1½ hours
Serves: 8 people

1 lb. large white beans
1½ qts. water
1 tsp. salt
3 large tomatoes
2 large white onions
2 cloves garlic
5 tbs. balsamic vinegar
3 pinches each sugar, salt, and freshly ground black pepper
6 tbs. cold-pressed olive oil
1 tsp. each thyme and chopped sage
6 rosemary needles

Rinse the beans and soak them in the water for 12 hours. • The next day, bring the beans to a boil in their soaking water and cook for 1½ hours, adding the salt only in the last minutes of cooking. • Rinse and quarter the tomatoes, remove all stem parts, then slice thinly. • Peel the onions and garlic, slice the onion into thin rings and chop the garlic. • Blend the vinegar, sugar, salt and pepper, then vigorously stir in the olive oil. Add the herbs. • Drain the beans. Combine with the other ingredients in a bowl and pour the dressing over the salad.

Rice Salad with Fruits

Easy to prepare

Preparation time: 50 minutes
Marinating time: 30 minutes
Serves: 8 people

lb. long grain rice
qt. water
tsp. salt
stalks celery
small pineapple
oranges
stalks chicory
handful basil
juice of 1 orange
tbs. lemon juice
tbs. corn oil
lb. yogurt
cup heavy cream
tsp. sugar

Pour the rice into the boiling, salted water and cook, covered, over low heat for 15 to 20 minutes. • Pull off the tough fibers of the celery, rinse, dry, and slice crosswise. • Peel the pineapple, quarter lengthwise, core, and dice. • Peel the oranges, segment, and halve the segments. • Remove the outer, decayed leaves from the chicory, rinse, dry, trim the root end and cut out the bitter wedge of the stem. Shred the chicory. • Rinse and dry the basil, remove stems and cut the leaves into strips. • Blend the orange juice, lemon juice, oil and yogurt, then toss with the fruits. Sprinkle the basil over the salad and marinate, covered, for 30 minutes. • Whip the cream with sugar until it is fairly stiff and serve separately.

Rice Salad with Peppers

Quick, easy to prepare

Preparation time: 40 minutes
Marinating time: 2 hours
Serves: 8 people

1 lb. long grain rice
1 qt. water
1 tsp. salt
1 large onion
3 large green bell peppers
12 stalks celery
8 tbs. tarragon vinegar
2 pinches black pepper
1 pinch cayenne pepper
1½ tsp. dried coriander
¼ tsp. ground nutmeg
8 tbs. safflower seed oil
½ lb. salted cashews

Pour the rice into the boiling salted water and simmer for 15 to 20 minutes. • Peel and chop the onion. • Halve the peppers, clean, rinse, and cut into thin strips. • Remove the tough fibers from the celery, rinse, and cut into ½ inch pieces. • Drain the rice well. • Blend the vinegar, pepper, cayenne, coriander, and nutmeg, then vigorously stir in the safflower seed oil. Toss the dressing with the rice and vegetables. • Marinate for 2 hours. • Add the cashews, then spice to taste and arrange on a platter before serving.

Vegetarian Potato Salad

Easy to prepare, a little expensive

Preparation: 45 minutes
Serves: 8 people

2 medium fennel bulbs
2 hearts of celery
6 medium-sized cooked potatoes
2 heads chicory
½ lb. Gruyère cheese
12 artichoke hearts (canned in oil)
½ lb. small, canned mushrooms
6 tbs. wine vinegar
3 pinches each salt and freshly ground black pepper
4 to 5 tbs. mayonnaise
2 tsp. capers
4 hard-boiled eggs
8 anchovy rings
3 tbs. freshly chopped parsley

Remove the stems and decayed leaves from the fennel bulbs. Rinse, dry, and slice the fennel into thin rings. • Rinse, dry, and slice the celery hearts. • Peel and dice the potatoes. • Remove the outer leaves of chicory, rinse the stalks and dry. Cut out the bitter wedge at the root end. Slice the chicory crosswise into thin strips. • Dice the cheese, drain the artichoke hearts and mushrooms, and halve or quarter them. • Blend the wine vinegar, salt, pepper, mayonnaise, and the chopped capers. • Toss all ingredients with the dressing. Arrange on plates. • Peel and chop the eggs, then scatter them over the servings. Garnish with the anchovy rings and parsley.

Potato Salad with Roast Meat

Inexpensive

Preparation time: 55 minutes
Marinating time: 10 minutes
Serves: 8 people

3 lbs. potatoes (should stay firm after cooking)
1 lb. leftover roast meat (beef, veal, or pork)
1 lb. celeriac (knob celery)
3 carrots
3 pickles
3 onions
1 handful parsley
8 tbs. red wine vinegar
1 tsp. each salt and freshly ground black pepper
8 tbs. herbal oil
2 hard-boiled eggs

Wash the potatoes and boil them in enough water to cover for about 30 minutes. • Dice the meat. Peel and rinse the celeriac, and julienne together with the peeled carrots. Dice the pickles. Peel the onions and cut them into rings. Wash and chop the parsley. • Blend the vinegar, salt and pepper, then vigorously whisk in the oil. • Pour off the water from the potatoes, peel, and slice them. • Combine the sliced potatoes with the prepared ingredients. Toss the salad with the dressing and marinate for 10 minutes. • Peel and chop the eggs, then scatter them over the salad.

Moroccan Orange Salad

Quick, inexpensive

Preparation time: 40 minutes
Marinating time: 1 hour
Serves: 8 people

cups long grain rice
tsp. salt
qt. water
medium oranges
small white onions
½ cup white wine
pinches salt
¼ lb. stuffed olives
tbs. vinegar
pinches black pepper
tbs. grated horseradish
pinch sugar
tbs. oil

Cook the rice in the salted water for about 15 minutes.
• Peel the oranges like apples, in order to remove the white inner skin. Skin the segments, reserving any juice. • Peel, halve, and slice the onions. Bring the white wine with ½ cup water and 1 pinch salt to a boil, and blanch the onions in this liquid for 3 minutes. Drain the onions, reserving any liquid. • Drain the rice, too. • Halve the olives and combine, in a large salad bowl, with the oranges, rice, and onions. • Blend the vinegar with 2 pinches salt, pepper, horseradish, sugar, 3 or 4 tablespoons of the onion broth, orange juice and oil. • Gently toss the dressing with the salad. • Marinate for at least 1 hour.

Corn Salad with Black Olives

Easy to prepare, inexpensive

Soaking time: 8 hours
Preparation time: 1¼ hours
Marinating time: 1 hour
Serves: 8 people

½ lb. small white beans
1 qt. water
½ tsp. salt
1 lb. canned corn
1 large onion
½ lb. feta cheese
1 handful parsley
1 cup black olives
1 or 2 cloves garlic
6 tbs. tarragon vinegar
2 pinches each salt and freshly ground white pepper
4 tbs. oil

Rinse the beans and soak them overnight in 1 quart of water. • The next day, cook the beans for 1 hour in their soaking water, adding the salt after 50 minutes. Drain the beans in a sieve. • Drain the corn. • Peel and chop the onion. Dice the feta. Rinse, dry and chop the parsley. • Drain the olives and combine them with the other ingredients in a large bowl. • Peel the garlic cloves, crush into a small bowl, then blend with the vinegar, salt and pepper. Add the oil, vigorously blend the dressing and pour it over the salad. • Toss the salad and marinate for 1 hour.

Herring Salad with Potatoes

Easy to prepare

Preparation time: 45 minutes
Marinating time: 30 minutes
Serves: 8 people

3 lbs. potatoes
6 pickled white (Matjes) herring fillets
2 large tart apples
2 onions
4 small cucumbers
½ cup hot beef broth
6 tbs. mayonnaise
½ lb. sour cream
4 tbs. herbal vinegar
2 tsp. freshly grated horseradish
1 tsp. each salt and freshly ground black pepper
2 pinches sugar
1 handful dill

Rinse the potatoes, then bring to a boil in enough water to cover and cook for 30 minutes. • If necessary, soak the herring fillets in water for 30 minutes. • Quarter, peel, core and dice the apples. Peel the onions and dice them together with the cucumbers. • Drain the potatoes, allow them to steam dry, peel and slice. • Pat the herring dry, dice, and combine with the potatoes, apples, onions, cucumbers and the beef broth. • Blend the mayonnaise with the sour cream, vinegar, horseradish, salt, pepper, and sugar. Rinse and chop the dill, and toss it with the dressing and the salad. • Marinate for 30 minutes.

Red Herring Salad

Takes some time

Preparation time: 1½ hours
Marinating time: 12 hours
Serves: 8 people

1½ lbs. red beets
12 pickled white (Matjes) herring fillets
1 lb. cold veal roast
½ lb. cooked ham
10 gherkins
3 tbs. small capers
6 tbs. mayonnaise
3 tbs. red wine vinegar
2 tbs. ketchup
2 pinches each salt and sugar
1 tsp. freshly ground black pepper
3 hard-boiled eggs

Brush the beets under running water. Bring 2 quarts water to a boil, add the beets and cook them, depending on their size, for 40 to 80 minutes. If necessary, soak the herring in water for 30 minutes. • Dice the veal, ham, and gherkins. Drain the capers and add to the diced ingredients. • Drain the herring, cut into strips, and add to the prepared ingredients. • Allow the beets to cool a little, then peel, dice and add them to the other ingredients. • Blend the mayonnaise, vinegar, ketchup, salt, sugar and pepper, then toss with the salad. • Marinate the salad, covered, overnight. • Season to taste before serving. Peel the eggs and cut them into eighths, then garnish the salad with them

Potato Salad with Red Beans

Easy to prepare, inexpensive

Preparation time: 55 minutes
Marinating time: 1 hour
Serves: 8 people

1 lb. potatoes
3 cups water
1 tsp. salt
2 cans kidney beans (about 1 lb. each)
½ lb. Emmenthaler cheese
3 onions
½ cup herbal vinegar
3 pinches each salt and freshly ground black pepper
2 tbs. marjoram leaves
9 tbs. sunflower seed oil
¼ lb. bacon

Brush the potatoes well under running water, then cook them in the salted water for about 30 minutes. Pour off the water, let the potatoes steam dry, then rinse them under cold water. Peel and dice the potatoes. • Rinse and drain the kidney beans. • Dice the cheese and add to the potatoes and beans. • Peel and chop the onions, then add them to the dressing made of the vinegar, salt, pepper, marjoram, and 8 tablespoons sunflower seed oil. Pour the sauce over the potatoes, beans and cheese and toss well. Marinate for 1 hour. • Dice the bacon and fry until it is golden brown in 1 tablespoon oil. Scatter the bacon bits over the salad.

Soybean Salad with Peppers

Nutritious

Soaking time: 12 hours
Cooking time: about 2 hours
Preparation time: 30 minutes
Marinating time: 20 minutes
Serves: 8 people

A little over ½ lb. yellow soybeans
1 lb. green bell peppers
1 tsp. salt
1 lb. tart apples
3 red onions
2 cups yogurt
6 tbs. olive oil
6 tbs. sherry vinegar
1 tbs. soy sauce
3 tsp. sweet paprika powder
1 tsp. sea salt
2 to 3 pinches freshly ground black pepper

Soak the beans overnight in 1 quart water. • The next day, cook the beans in their soaking water for about 2 hours, then drain. • Rinse, quarter, and trim the peppers, removing all stem parts, ribs and seeds, then cut into thin strips. Blanch the peppers for about 30 seconds in boiling water and drain. • Rinse, dry, quarter, core and dice the apples. • Peel and halve the onions, then slice thinly. • Blend the yogurt, oil, vinegar, soy sauce, and paprika powder, then combine with the prepared ingredients. Salt and pepper to taste and marinate for at least 20 minutes.

Judic Salad

Famous recipe

Preparation time: 1 hour
Serves: 8 people

| 4 lbs. potatoes |
| 1 lb. carrots |
| 1 small head cauliflower |
| 1 lb. small Brussels sprouts |
| ½ qt. milk |
| ½ qt. water |
| 1 lb. green beans |
| 1 pinch salt |
| 2 medium red beets |
| 5 tbs. capers |
| 2 onions |
| 3 to 4 tbs. white wine vinegar |
| 1 tsp. salt |
| ½ tsp. white pepper |
| 6 tbs. olive oil |
| 1 handful each tarragon and chervil |
| 2 handfuls chives |

Brush the potatoes well und
running water, then cook i
enough water to cover for 30
minutes. • Peel, rinse, and dice
the carrots. • Cut off the florets
from the cauliflower (save the
stems for a soup). Rinse the florets and drain. Halve the larger
florets. • Cook the vegetables in
the water and milk for about 15
minutes. • Clean and trim the
green beans. Cook the beans in
just enough salted water to cove
for 15 minutes. • Drain the
cooked vegetables in a sieve. •
Brush the beets under running
water, peel, and coarsely grate.
Chop the capers. Peel and cho
the onions. • Drain the potatoe
let them steam dry, peel and
dice. • Blend the white wine vin
egar with the capers, onions, sa
and pepper, then vigorously stir
in the oil. • Combine the potatoes, vegetables, beets and
dressing. • Rinse, chop, and
sprinkle the herbs over the salad

Confetti Salad

Inexpensive, easy to prepare

Preparation time: 40 minutes
Marinating time: 30 minutes
Serves: 8 people

lb. risotto
qt. water
½ tsp. salt
oz. canned corn
red bell peppers
carrots
pinches salt
lb. frozen peas
⅓ lb. Gouda cheese
onions
clove garlic
small zucchini
tbs. (fruit-based) vinegar
tsp. each salt and white pepper
tbs. wheat seed oil
handful chives

Rinse the rice several times, then bring the salted water to a boil, pour in the rice and cook over low heat for 20 minutes. • Drain the corn. • Halve the peppers, remove all stem parts, seeds, and ribs, rinse, dry and dice. • Peel, rinse, and dice the carrots. Cook them in salted water for 10 minutes. After 5 minutes add the peas and cook them with the carrots. • Dice the Gouda. • Peel and chop the onions and garlic. • Trim, rinse, dry, and dice the zucchini. • Blend the vinegar, salt, pepper, and oil. • Drain the rice, let cool, and combine with the other ingredients and the dressing. • Chop the chives and sprinkle over the salad.

Vegetable-Rice Salad

Inexpensive, easy to prepare

Preparation time: 45 minutes
Serves: 8 people

1 lb. long grain rice
1 qt. water
½ tsp. salt
3 carrots
½ lb. Emmenthaler cheese
⅔ lb. celery
1 handful spring onions
5 tbs. mayonnaise
⅔ lb. yogurt
4 tbs. white wine vinegar
1 tsp. each herbal salt and freshly ground white pepper
1 pinch cayenne pepper
1 handful each dill, parsley, and chives
A few attractive leaves of Boston lettuce

Pour the rice into the boiling, salted water, then cook for 20 minutes over low heat. • Peel and rinse the carrots, then cook them with the rice for 15 minutes. • Cut the cheese into fine strips. • Remove any tough fibers from the celery, if necessary. Rinse, dry, and thinly slice the celery. Chop a little of the celery greens. Trim, rinse, and cut the root ends from the spring onions, then cut them into rings. • Slice the carrots. Drain the rice and allow to cool. • Blend the mayonnaise, yogurt, vinegar, salt, pepper, and cayenne. Rinse, dry and chop the herbs, then add them and the celery greens to the yogurt dressing. • Combine the rice with the prepared ingredients. Toss the salad with the dressing and arrange on the lettuce leaves.

Fruits of the Sea Salad

Somewhat more expensive, easy to prepare

Preparation time: 50 minutes
Serves: 8 people

3 lbs. cod
2 tbs. lemon juice
1 cup water
2 sprigs parsley
½ bay leaf
2 pinches salt
½ tsp. white peppercorns
¼ lb. long grain rice
1½ cups chicken broth
1 ripe mango
Juice of 1 lemon
⅔ lb. crème fraîche
2 tsp. grated horseradish
1 tsp. sugar
1 pinch freshly ground white pepper
⅔ lb. small shrimp, cooked
⅔ lb. smoked shark fillet
A few leaves of lettuce
1 tsp. red peppercorns
A few sprigs of lemon balm

Rinse the cod and sprinkle the lemon juice over it. Bring the water with the parsley, bay leaf, salt and pepper to a boil. Poach the fish, covered, over low heat for 15 to 20 minutes. • Cook the rice in the chicken broth for 15 to 20 minutes and drain. • Peel the mango and blend with the lemon juice, crème fraîche, horseradish, and a little broth from the fish to obtain a thick dressing. Add sugar and pepper to taste. • Separate the fish into small pieces, rinse and drain the shrimp, cut the shark into strips and combine all three with the rice. • Arrange the salad on the lettuce leaves, pour the dressing over it, and garnish with peppercorns and lemon balm.

Brown Rice Salad with Fish

Nutritious recipe

Preparation time: 1 hour
Marinating time: 20 minutes
Serves: 8 people

¾ cup rice
2 cups water
2 tsp. granulated vegetable broth
1½ lb. salmon fillet
1 tbs. lemon juice
1 tsp. salt
1 lb. celeriac (knob celery)
1 qt. water
1 tsp. salt
2 egg yolks
1 tbs. each soy sauce, mustard, and honey
½ tsp. black pepper
1 tsp. curry powder
4 tbs. safflower seed oil
1½ cups sour cream
Just under 1 lb. pineapple
2 tbs. each chopped chives and chopped dill

Cook the rice with the water and the granulated vegetable broth for 20 minutes. Rinse the fish, lay onto the rice, sprinkle with lemon juice and salt, then cook over low heat for another 15 minutes. Allow the rice to cool, separate the fish into pieces, removing any bones you might find. • Peel and rinse the celeriac, then cut into thin strips. Blanch in the salted water for 2 minutes and drain. • Blend the egg yolks with the soy sauce, mustard, honey, pepper, and curry, then slowly stir in the oil. Add half of the sour cream to the dressing, then toss with the prepared ingredients. • Marinate for 20 minutes. • Dice the pineapple and add it to the salad, together with the remaining sour cream and the herbs.

otato-Pumpkin alad

omewhat more expensive, asy to prepare

eparation time: 55 minutes arinating time: 30 minutes erves: 8 people

lbs. potatoes
lb. pickled pumpkin
lb. small shrimp (canned)
tart apples
shallots
ice of 1 lemon
cup hot chicken broth
cups sour cream
tbs. chopped dill
pinches salt
handfuls garden cress

Brush the potatoes well under running water, bring to a boil in enough water to cover and cook for 25 to 30 minutes. • Drain the pumpkin. Rinse the shrimp and drain. • Quarter, core, peel and dice the apples. Peel and chop the shallots. • Blend the lemon juice, chicken broth, sour cream, and dill. • Drain the potatoes, let cool, peel and slice. Combine the potatoes with the shrimp, pumpkin, apple, shallots, and cream dressing. Salt to taste. • Rinse, chop, and toss the cress with the salad. • Marinate, covered, for 30 minutes.

Potato Salad with Corn

Inexpensive, easy to prepare

Preparation time: 50 minutes
Marinating time: 1 hour
Final preparation: 15 minutes
Serves: 8 people

4 lbs. potatoes
3 medium onions
1 cup beef broth
½ cup vinegar
4 tsp. sugar
½ tsp. salt
1 pinch freshly ground white pepper
2 tbs. mayonnaise
1¼ cups sour cream
1 tsp. hot mustard
4 tbs. lemon juice
10 oz. canned corn
10 oz. peas (fresh or frozen)
2 red bell peppers

1 handful each dill and parsley

Wash the potatoes and cook in enough water to cover for 20 to 25 minutes. • Peel and chop the onions, then bring them together with the broth, vinegar, 3 teaspoons sugar, salt and pepper to a boil and remove from heat. • Blend the mayonnaise, sour cream, mustard, lemon juice, and 1 tsp. sugar. • Peel and slice the potatoes, then pour the hot vinegar broth over them. Marinate for 1 hour. • Drain the corn. Rinse fresh peas in cold water, frozen peas in hot water and drain. Halve the bell peppers, remove all stem parts, ribs and seeds, rinse and dice. Rinse the dill and parsley, dry, and chop. • Toss the vegetables, herbs and dressing with the potatoes.

Iceberg Lettuce with Chicken and Mango Dressing

Easy to prepare, inexpensive

Preparation time: 50 minutes
Serves: 8 people

1 chicken breast (a little over ½ lb.)
1 cup water
¼ tsp. salt
2 pinches freshly ground white pepper
1 small bay leaf
1 small head iceberg lettuce
2 slices fresh pineapple
1 lb. celery
2 tbs. walnuts
4 tbs. mayonnaise
6 tbs. mango sauce
1 cup crème fraîche
1 pinch salt
1 tsp. lemon juice
A few dashes Worcestershire sauce

Rinse the chicken, then cook in the salted water, together with the bay leaf and 1 pinch pepper for 15 minutes over low heat. • Meanwhile, separate the leaves of lettuce, discarding any decayed or unattractive leaves. Rinse and dry. Tear the leaves into small pieces. • Peel and core the pineapple slices. Cut the pineapple into thin wedges. • If necessary, remove any tough fibers from the celery, rinse the stalks, and slice lengthwise. • Coarsely chop the walnuts. • Remove the chicken from the broth, and skin and bone the breast. Cube the meat and combine with the other ingredients while still warm. • Blend the mayonnaise, mango sauce, crème fraîche, 1 pinch pepper, salt and lemon juice, then add Worcestershire sauce to taste. Pour the dressing over the salad and toss gently. • Marinate briefly.

New Year's Salad

Takes some time

Soaking time: 1 hour
Preparation time: 1 hour
Marinating time: 3 to 4 hours
Serves: 8 people

6 pickled white (Matjes) herring fillets

½ lb. celeriac (knob celery)

1 bay leaf

1 pinch salt

1 lb. cooked beef

1 lb. cooked potatoes

½ lb. pickled beets

2 small cucumbers

2 onions

1 lb. celeriac

1 large tart apple

½ lb. mayonnaise

⅔ lb. sour cream

1 tsp. vinegar

2 pinches each salt and freshly ground white pepper

1 tsp. mustard

3 hard-boiled eggs

A few nice leaves of lettuce

1 handful parsley

Soak the herring in cold water for 1 hour. • Peel, rinse and cook whole, in enough water to cover, with the bay leaf and salt, for 20 minutes. • Dice the beef, potatoes, red beets, and cucumbers. • Peel and chop the onions. • Peel, quarter, core, and dice the apple. • Drain the celeriac and dice. • Pat dry the herring and cut into pieces. • Blend the mayonnaise, sour cream, vinegar, salt, pepper, and mustard. Toss the salad with the dressing and marinate 3 to 4 hours. • Peel the eggs and cut them into eighths. Arrange the salad on plates and garnish with the eggs and parsley.

Belgian Egg Salad

Inexpensive, easy to prepare

Preparation time: 50 minutes
Marinating time: 1 hour
Serves: 8 people

Just under ½ lb. mayonnaise

2 tsp. tomato paste

3 tbs. lemon juice

6 to 8 tbs. water

1 small onion

2 pinches each salt and pepper

½ tsp. sugar

8 medium, cooked potatoes

2 small cucumbers

2 apples

4 medium heads chicory

1 bunch radishes

10 hard-boiled eggs

Blend the mayonnaise, tomato paste, lemon juice, and water. Peel the onion and grate it into the dressing. Add salt, pepper, and sugar to taste. • Peel the potatoes and make ½ inch cubes. • Finely dice the cucumbers. Peel, core and slice the apples. • Combine the potatoes, cucumbers and apples with the dressing and marinate for 1 hour. • Rinse the chicory, remove the tips of the leaves, and shred the chicory. • Rinse and slice the radishes. • Peel the eggs and cut each into 6 wedges. • Toss the salad with the chicory and radishes. Garnish with the eggs and tips of chicory leaves.

Mushroom Salad in Honeydew Melon

Easy to prepare

Preparation time: 30 minutes
Serves: 8 people

10 oz. frozen peas
1 lb. mushrooms
⅓ lb. lightly smoked and lightly salted pork
4 honeydew melons
5 tbs. lemon juice
1 tsp. salt
2 pinches each sugar and freshly ground white pepper
2 tbs. dry sherry
4 tbs. wheat seed oil
2 tbs. green peppercorns

Cook the peas in 1 cup water for 5 minutes. • Clean, rinse, dry, and thinly slice the mushrooms. • Cut the ham into thin strips. • Halve the honeydews, spoon out the seeds, and take out the flesh with a melon baller. • Blend the lemon juice, salt, pepper, sugar, sherry, and oil. Combine the cooled peas, prepared ingredients, dressing and peppercorns. • Arrange the salad in the melon halves and refrigerate, covered, until time to serve.

Shrimp Salad

Somewhat more expensive

Preparation time: 1 hour
Serves: 8 people

1 small head each of iceberg, romaine, and radicchio lettuce
½ large cucumber
½ lb. small sweet tomatoes
5 stalks celery
2 spring onions
¼ lb. small mushrooms
2 medium oranges
1 can of lichees (10 oz.)
1 lb. cooked shrimp
2 cups sour cream
6 tbs. mayonnaise
4 tbs. dill vinegar
2 tbs. ketchup
½ tsp. salt
2 pinches freshly ground white pepper
1 pinch cayenne pepper
2 handfuls dill

Clean the lettuce, rinse, separate the leaves and dry. Tear the iceberg leaves into smaller pieces, shred the radicchio and romaine. • Peel and coarsely grate the cucumber. • Rinse, quarter and core the tomatoes. • Rinse the celery, remove any tough fibers, if necessary, and cut lengthwise. • Clean the spring onions and mushrooms, rinse and slice. • Peel the oranges and skin the segments. • Combine all prepared ingredients in a large bowl. Drain the lichees. Halve the fruits and add to the salad with the shrimp. • Blend the sour cream, mayonnaise, vinegar, ketchup, salt, pepper, and cayenne. Rinse, dry, and mince the dill and fold into the dressing. Add juice from the lichees to the dressing to taste and toss with the salad. Serve with French bread and butter.

Egg and Potato Salad with Herring Dressing

Inexpensive, easy to prepare

Preparation time: 1 hour
Marinating time: 30 minutes
Serves: 8 people

2 lbs. potatoes
10 eggs
4 pickled white (Matjes) herring fillets
1 ⅓ cups cottage or ricotta cheese
½ lb. cream
2 pinches salt
1 tsp. freshly ground white pepper
1 handful chives

Brush the potatoes well under running water, then bring to a boil in enough water to cover and cook for 30 minutes. • Pierce the eggs at the round end, lay into boiling water and cook for 8 minutes. Briefly rinse the eggs in cold water. • Puree the herring in a blender and blend with the fresh cheese, cream, salt and pepper. • Drain the potatoes, steam dry, peel, slice, and toss with the herring cream. • Peel the eggs, cut them into eighths, and toss with the salald. • Rinse the chives, dry, chop and sprinkle over the salad. • Marinate for 30 minutes.

Tip: You can make this salad well ahead of time. Just remember to add the eggs and chives right before serving the salad.

Whole-Grain Pasta Salad

Nutritious, quick

Preparation time: 40 minutes
Marinating time: 10 minutes
Serves: 8 people

10 cardamom seeds
2 qts. water
2 tsp. salt
⅔ lb. whole-grain pasta (spirelli)
2 oz. unpeeled sesame seeds
⅔ cup cream
4 tbs. lemon juice
2 tbs. each soy sauce and sesame seed oil
2 to 3 tsp. curry powder
½ tsp. Indian saffron
½ tsp. freshly ground white pepper
3 lbs. pineapple
6 bananas
3 tbs. chopped chives

Make an incision in the cardamom seeds and bring to a boil in the salted water. Cook the noodles in boiling water for 12 to 15 minutes, drain and allow to cool. • Roast the sesame seeds in a pan until they begin to pop and have a pleasant aroma. Put the seeds aside. • Blend a dressing of the cream, lemon juice, oil, soy sauce, curry powder, saffron, and pepper. • About 20 minutes before serving the salad, peel the pineapple, quarter lengthwise, core, and then dice the fruit. • Peel and slice the bananas. • Combine the drained noodles, pineapple, banana, sesame seeds, dressing, and chives. Marinate for 10 minutes and add curry and pepper to taste.

Soybean Noodle Salad

Quick

Soaking time: 12 hours
Preparation time: 40 minutes
Marinating time: 10 minutes
Serves: 8 people

½ lb. mottled beans
1 bay leaf
1 tbs. mixed dried herbs
½ lb. noodles
2 qts. water
½ tsp. salt
½ lb. red onions
½ lb. salami
½ cup red wine vinegar
2 tsp. each sea salt and paprika powder
1 tsp. freshly ground black pepper
½ cup olive oil
2 tbs. freshly chopped parsley

Soak the beans overnight in 1 quart water. • Cook the beans in their soaking water with the bay leaf and dried herbs for about 30 minutes, then drain in a sieve and remove the bay leaf. • Meanwhile, cook the noodles in the boiling salted water 10 to 15 minutes, pour into a sieve, rinse, and drain. • Peel and halve the onions lengthwise, then slice. Cut the salami into thin strips. • Blend the vinegar, sea salt, paprika and pepper, then beat in the olive oil. Toss the ingredients with the dressing. • Marinate for 10 minutes. Toss in the parsley.

Danish Elbow Macaroni Salad

Easy to prepare, inexpensive

Preparation time: 55 minutes
Marinating time: 1 hour
Serves: 8 people

| 1 lb. small elbow macaroni |
| 2½ tsp. salt |
| 2 tbs. oil |
| 5 carrots |
| ½ lb. celeriac (knob celery) |
| 1 lb. frozen peas |
| 1 lb. cooked ham (without fatty rind) |
| 1 large pineapple |
| 3 onions |
| 1 lb. mayonnaise |
| 6 tbs. lemon juice |
| 3 pinches each salt and freshly ground white pepper |
| A few dashes of Worcestershire sauce |
| 4 tbs. chopped chives |

Cook the noodles in 2 quarts water with 2 teaspoons salt and the oil for 10 to 12 minutes, then drain. • Peel and rinse the carrots and celeriac, then cook in a little water with ½ teaspon salt for 15 minutes. Remove the vegetables, slice the carrots, dice the celeriac. • Parboil the frozen peas in the vegetable broth and drain. • Dice the ham. • Peel, core and dice the pineapple. Reserve any juice. • Peel and chop the onions, then combine with the other ingredients. • Blend the mayonnaise, pineapple and lemon juice, salt, pepper, and a few dashes of Worcestershire sauce, then toss the dressing and the chives with the salad. Marinate 1 hour.

Green Spaghetti Salad

Easy to prepare, quick

Preparation time: 15 minutes
Marinating time: 1 hour
Serves: 8 people

| 4 qts. water |
| 2 tsp. salt |
| 1 lb. green spaghetti |
| 8 to 10 tbs. fresh mixed herbs: parsley, chervil, lemon balm, pimpernel |
| 8 tbs. tarragon vinegar |
| 8 to 10 tbs. olive oil |
| 4 cloves garlic |
| 4 shallots |
| ¼ lb. freshly grated Parmesan cheese |
| ½ tsp. freshly ground white pepper |
| 3 to 4 oz. pine nuts |

Bring the salted water to a boil. Break in the spaghetti (the pieces should be about 4 inches long), and cook for about 8 minutes. Drain the noodles. • Rinse the herbs, remove tough stems, and puree with the vinegar and oil in a blender. • Peel and chop the shallots and garlic, then add to the pureed herbs. Add the Parmesan and pepper to taste. • Combine the puree with the pasta and pine nuts. Marinate for 1 hour. • Arrange the salad on a platter and serve with small hamburgers or veal steaks.

Italian Pasta Salad

Easy to prepare, somewhat expensive

Preparation time: 50 minutes
Serves: 8 people

4 qts. water
2 tsp. salt
1 lb. white and green spiral noodles (spirelli)
2 lbs. tomatoes
1 lb. cold veal rost
2 tbs. capers
2 tbs. pine nuts
2 handfuls basil
8 tbs. mayonnaise
2 tbs. red wine vinegar
⅔ lb. yogurt
1 tsp. each salt and freshly ground black pepper

Bring the salted water to a boil. Cook the pasta in the water for about 8 minutes, until "al dente," then drain and let cool. • Make a crosswise cut on the bottoms of the tomatoes, briefly parboil, halve, peel, and remove seeds and stem parts. Dice the tomatoes. • Dice the veal and combine with the capers, pine nuts, tomato, and drained pasta. • Rinse, dry, and cut the basil into strips. Save some basil leaves for garnish. • Combine the basil with the mayonnaise, vinegar, yogurt, salt and pepper. • Toss the salad with the dressing and garnish with the basil leaves.

Pasta Salad with Salami and Cheese

Inexpensive, easy to prepare

Preparation time: 50 minutes
Serves: 8 people

4 qts. water
2 tsp. salt
1 lb. shell pasta
⅔ lb. Tilsiter cheese
½ lb. thinly sliced salami
4 hard-boiled eggs
2 red bell peppers
2 bunches radishes
6 tbs. red wine vinegar
1 tsp. salt
1 tsp. freshly ground black pepper
½ tsp. sweet red paprika powder
5 tbs. cold-pressed olive oil

Bring the salted water to a boil and cook the pasta in it until "al dente," drain, rinse and let cool. • Cut the cheese and salami into thin strips. Peel the eggs and cut them into eighths. • Halve the bell peppers, remove all seeds, ribs and stem parts, rinse, dry, and dice. • Clean the radishes, rinse, dry, put aside a few for garnish, and slice the rest. • Blend the vinegar, salt, pepper, and paprika powder, then stir in the oil. • Combine the cold noodles, cheese, salami, diced peppers, radish slices and dressing. • Decoratively cut the remaining radishes and garnish the salad. Marinate, covered, until time to serve.

Spaghetti Salad with Roast Beef

Easy to prepare, somewhat expensive

Preparation time: 40 minutes
Marinating time: 15 minutes
Serves: 8 people

lb. spaghetti	
qts. water	
tsp. salt	
large cucumber	
½ tsp. each salt and freshly ground white pepper	
tbs. balsamic vinegar	
lb. small tomatoes	
bunches radishes	
½ lb. cold pork roast	
lb. cold roast beef	
small onions	
pinches sweet paprika powder	
dashes Tabasco sauce	
tbs. olive oil	

Cook the noodles until "al dente" (about 8 minutes), in the boiling salted water. • Peel and dice the cucumber, sprinkle ¼ teaspoon salt and pepper and 1 tablespoon vinegar over it. • Peel and halve the tomatoes, then cut the halves into thirds. • Clean, rinse, and slice the radishes. Cut the roast pork and beef into strips. • Pour off any liquid from the cucumber. • Peel and chop the onions. • Blend a dressing of 7 tablespoons vinegar, ¼ teaspoon each of salt and pepper, paprika powder, Tabasco sauce, olive oil, and the chopped onions. Toss with the salad ingredients. • Marinate, covered and refrigerated, for 15 minutes.

Pasta Salad with Mussels

Takes some time

Preparation time: 1½ hours
Serves: 8 people

4 lbs. mussels	
2 cloves garlic	
4 sprigs parsley	
2 cups dry white wine	
½ lb. peas	
½ cup vegetable broth	
6 tomatoes	
½ lb. canned tuna	
⅔ lb. small shrimp, cooked	
2 tbs. capers	
10 tbs. olive oil	
Juice of 2 lemons	
1 lb. spiral noodles	
2½ tsp. salt	
3 pinches freshly ground black pepper	

Brush the mussels well under running water and remove their "beards." Peel and crush the garlic, then cook, covered, with the parsley, mussels, and wine for 10 minutes. Shake the pot occasionally. Discard unopened mussels. Remove the mussels from their shells. • Cook the peas in the vegetable broth for 10 minutes and drain. • Peel and dice the tomatoes. • Pull the tuna into small pieces. Combine 8 tablespoons oil and the lemon juice with the mussels, shrimp, peas, tomatoes, and capers. Marinate, refrigerated, for 30 minutes. • Cook the pasta "al dente" in 4 quarts water with 2 teaspoons salt. Toss 2 tablespoons olive oil with the drained spaghetti. Combine the salad and pasta, adding ½ teaspoon salt and pepper.

Index